THE MOST UNBELIEVABLE HOCKEY STORIES FOR YOUNG READERS

21 Inspirational Tales Every Fan Should Know - Discover Incredible Hockey Facts About The All-Time Greats

FENIX PUBLISHING

"For every hockey fan, from young pucksters
to seasoned veterans, may this book be a source of inspiration
and admiration for the remarkable stories that shape the heart
and soul of our beloved game."

Want **FREE BOOKS** for the rest of your LIFE?

Join our VIP club now by scanning the QR code to get **FREE** access to all our future books or enter this link: bit.ly/Free-Hockey-Books into your search browser.

We **ONLY** send you an email when we launch a **NEW BOOK. NO SPAM.** Never. Ever!

Just an email with **YOUR 100% OFF COUPON CODE.**

TABLE OF CONTENTS

YOUR OPINION MATTERS TO US!

We've poured our hearts and souls into this project and ensured that every fact is well-researched, reviewed, and accurate. We would love to hear what you think about this book and how it has inspired you as a hockey lover. We would appreciate the support and critical analysis you provide so that we can confidently and energetically continue the work we love.

The objective of the book is to present information that is true and safe for our younger readers, with 100% accuracy, to enhance your knowledge about hockey: a game we are incredibly passionate about at our small publishing company. When you provide us with feedback, we can improve the content and better meet your expectations, and that is why your engagement with us is so important.

Your reviews will help us understand how to give you a better quality of reading enjoyment and motivate us to keep producing high-quality material for everyone who is passionate about hockey.

INTRODUCTION

Bravery is facing the challenges you fear and overcoming them with hard work, perseverance, and dedication to your craft. It means following in the footsteps of people who have walked the path before you. It signifies feeling the butterflies of nerves, lacing up those boots, and sliding out on the ice to the cheers of thousands. It's owning your place among the giants, even if this means pretending that you're wearing your hero's number on your back and wielding his stick in your hands.

Being a part of something as magnificent as the ice hockey community is an honor that many young men and women have experienced. Some of them have become influential superstars with illustrious careers, while others had to bid an early goodbye because of injuries or other reasons.

IN THE BEGINNING

To understand any craft, you need to understand where it started, why it was created, and how it changed into the sport that we've come to love today.

Ice hockey is primarily enjoyed by people living in the northern hemisphere—especially in Europe, Canada, and North America—although it also finds a fan base throughout the globe. This is encouraged by the *Global Series* hosted by the National Hockey League (NHL), which took place in Melbourne, Australia with the LA Kings and Arizona Coyotes as the main hosts. To gain that status, hockey needed to have had a beginning.

Just like rugby had its origins in soccer and American football is descended from rugby, ice hockey was a product of a mixture of sports, with historians not sure exactly how it transformed into the game we know.

The one thing that most agree on is that hockey was popular from the very beginning, though the origins are filled with rumors. If taken as a whole, each rumor must have some truth when we see bits of the other sports on the ice. One rumor is that field hockey and lacrosse married, brought to Canada by British soldiers in the 1800s. Then there is evidence found in the Mi'kmaq Indian communities of a game that was distinctive to hockey—the sticks that were similar to those used in the Irish game of *hurling* teamed with a block of wood used as a ball. "Face-off" has its origins from the field hockey start-off known as *bully*, as well as the practice of hitting your opponent on the shins with your stick.

Ice hockey wasn't originally named as such, but was rather known as *shinty* because of the brutality of the game, often resulting in split shins and other injuries. Hockey was coined from the French term *hoquet* when the sport became more formalized. *Rink* was borrowed from the Scottish game of *curling*, and the first *puck* was dropped in Kingston Harbour, Canada, in 1860.

PRESENT DAY

The years between 1875 and 1908 were extremely important in the development of the formal leagues that are found today, with the first indoor game being recorded in Montreal in 1875, between two teams from McGill University. The McGill University Hockey Club originated from there in 1877. The *Amateur Hockey Association* (AHA) had four teams on their roster in 1885, with Queen's University winning the first championship with a 3-1 win.

The early 1900s saw the introduction of safety gear, including chest protectors (for goaltenders) and shin pads. The first official cup was donated by the governor-general of Canada—Sir Frederick Arthur, Lord Stanley of Preston—and awarded to the Montreal Amateur Athletic Association as the first winner of the *Stanley Cup* for the 1892-93 season. The Stanley Cup became the main prize of the NHL in 1926.

J. L. Gibson—a dentist who owned the Portage Lakers in Houghton, Michigan—brought Canadian players over in 1903, forming the first professional hockey team. This led to the formation of the *International Pro Hockey League* in 1904. Canada became the center of hockey when the *Ontario Professional Hockey League* was formed in 1908.

THE GLOBAL INFLUENCE

In 2016, the *International Ice Hockey Federation* (IIHF) recorded 1.64 million players in the formal aspect of the game, with over 40% of them coming from Canada—more players than the US, even though it has a population 10 times smaller. These numbers do not include the ever-increasing numbers of players from Finland, Sweden, the Czech Republic, Germany, France, Russia, and Iceland being drafted into the NHL. Many of these countries have also brought advances to the game in not just talent but in speed, accuracy, sportsmanship, and technique. Examples that naturally come to mind are Peter Forsberg and Erik Karlsson from Sweden, Jaromir Jagr from the Czech Republic, Tuukka Rask from Finland, and Anže Kopitar from Slovenia.

Each of these legends, and many more, have brought invaluable resources into the game, inspiring respect, enthusiasm, and many generations of future players. They were the role models that many young men and women fashioned their careers on. Each of them brought a part of themselves to the game: good, bad, or game-changing.

BETWEEN THESE PAGES

Now that the history has been dealt with, we will speak about the names that have changed the face of ice hockey in all its facets. The players mentioned on these pages are just a few of the outstanding athletes who give more than 100% to perfect their technique, improve their speed, practice their shots, and maintain their equipment—and in some cases, even add their trademark to the tools of the trade.

Each story will focus on the athlete's background, who they were before they were drafted, the challenges they faced during their careers, as well as their highs and lows, and how they worked their way to becoming the paragons of the sport. We will find out how Stan Mikita came to the "eureka" moment of creating the curved stick and how Connor Bedard recovered from injury to be the first draft pick of the 2023-24 season. We'll find out what helped Mario Lemieux become victorious over cancer.

We'll highlight game-changers such as Willie O'Ree, who broke the color barrier to become the first black player in the NHL. We'll talk about how Mattias Weinhandl's impact on hockey inspired other blind players to enjoy the game. We'll discuss the records made, and broken, by players.

We will also highlight the driving forces behind some of the most powerful teams around the world—the coaches—and their passion, methods, and the results they achieve as leaders, teachers, and mentors.

Throughout this book, you will find stories that inspire you, drive you, amuse you, and also encourage you to keep fighting, no matter the challenges you're facing. Find guidance from the legends you can look up to, discovering what you can and should do, and what you should avoid in your playing career. You will find guidance from each of the 21 athletes mentioned in this book. And maybe, one day, your name will be among theirs.

CHAPTER 1

STAN MIKITA —
THE INVENTOR OF THE CURVED STICK

*"Some of the most fun moments I've ever had in sports,
or in anything, were the games that Stan Mikita and I played
together with the Chicago Blackhawks."*
— Bobby Hull

Let's meet the man who designed the way hockey is played the world over.

Stan Mikita was born Stanislav Gouth on May 20th, 1940, in a tiny village in Sokolce in the Slovak Republic. He was taken to Canada as an 8-year-old, where he was adopted by his aunt, and his name was changed to Stanley Mikita. Not being able to speak a word of English, Stan struggled to adjust to his new life and dreamed of ways he could get back to his own country. He became interested in hockey when he watched some neighborhood boys playing. And that is how Stan learned how to speak English.

From the moment he picked up a stick, Stan was unstoppable on the ice. Entering the Ontario Hockey Association (OHA) to play for the St. Catherine Tepees, Stan quickly gained recognition and praise for his astonishing stick work, speed, and accuracy. He was drafted by the Chicago Blackhawks in 1958, won the Stanley Cup in 1961, and retired in 1980 after winning numerous trophies in his career.

Stan changed the course of history when he—accidentally and fundamentally—changed the most important piece of equipment needed to play hockey.

THE MI'KMAQ

The Mi'kmaqs played a vital role in the rumors of the origins of hockey when they played a game using L-shaped sticks made of hornbeam trees and a ball in the 1700s. The summers in eastern Canada were as vibrant as they were short, and the players started playing their game on ice to enjoy it in winter.

A hundred years later, hockey sticks were widely produced by the Starr Manufacturing Company—and another hundred years later, the mighty hockey stick was mass-produced. The 1950s strengthened the designs of the previous decade that changed the stick from a single unit into two or three pieces by adding fiberglass to the blades and shafts. This made them stronger and more durable.

This brings us to Stan's fortunate mishap in 1962, during a vigorous practice session. Rushing to get on the ice, he accidentally banged his stick into the bench door. Instead of taking the time to retrieve another stick, Stan continued to practice with his new, V-shaped stick. Despite the skeptical glances from his teammates, Stan found his crooked stick improved his shooting performance!

The puck will move either left or right when struck with the straight blade, making it harder to be accurate and causing you to expend more energy when making the shot. When using a curved blade, the puck is held within a shell that allows you to concentrate on *how* you use your stick rather than *where* your shot is going.

The more curved the blade is, the higher you can lift the puck over your opponent's stick, or over the goalie's padding to score. This doesn't automatically mean that you will be more accurate because not all shots will go where you want them to go, unless you work incredibly hard to control your puck movement.

STAN'S UPWARD CURVE

While using the straight stick, Stan had scored 27 goals during the 1958-59, 1959-60, and 1960-61 seasons with 52 assists. His first season in the NHL, he scored only 8 goals and 18 assists. His second season showed the grace and agility that he was known for since childhood, and he was able to score 19 goals with 34 assists.

Stan's scoring history was excellent but he barely featured in the top 10 scorers of the league... until he broke his stick. Renowned for his accuracy with a straight stick, Stan became unstoppable with a newly-innovated curved stick. With teammate Bobby Hull, they both ranked numbers 1 and 2 in the top 10 for an astonishing 8 seasons after taking steps to deliberately warp their tools. This upward trajectory earned Stan the Hart Trophy, the Art Ross Trophy, as well as the Lady Byng Trophy—for 2 years running. His game points also shot up by 24 points per season, remaining in the upper 70s and higher until the 1971 season.

Stan and Bobby reportedly soaked their sticks in warm water before hooking it under their hotel room doors overnight. There were also reports that Stan would borrow a blow torch from the maintenance crews to bend his sticks before going on the ice.

Stan was the player who wasn't afraid to push trends, especially when it concerned the benefits of the game or his safety. Witnessing the way the curved stick influenced Stan's shooting ability, other players started using it, as well. This is the time to remember, though, that hockey wasn't as padded and protected as it is today; with players not being able to control their shots as well as Stan, things were wild as unpredictable, crazy shots could end up injuring other players. With the curved stick, as we mentioned, you still need to control the shot, and this takes skill and accuracy.

During the 1969-70 season, the NHL ruled that the curve may not be more than an inch. This is in part to ensure fairness on the ice and that no player has an added advantage. The rule also ensured that players were safer on the ice. Stan and Bobby had recorded speeds of 120 mph with the new curved blades, "terrorizing" goaltenders throughout the league.

Besides being a danger to the goaltenders, eye injuries increased, as well. As the speeds of the wrist shots and slap shots became more advanced, the NHL regulated the curvature to half an inch, until about 2006 when it changed to three-fourths of an inch.

Modern players enjoyed the new depth, but some felt that the more curve the stick had, the more you would struggle to maintain control of the puck. Players often try to find loopholes and have been found to play with larger-than-regulation curves until the third period, to avoid the penalties. Marty McSorley was penalized for two minutes when the opposing team brought attention to the measurement of his stick during the 1993 Stanley Cup finals. This led to McSorley's team losing during overtime, and the other team going on to win the series.

This innovation gave the game great advancement, making it faster and more precise, and ensuring that players are skilled with puck control and their footwork. It allowed for more goals, more assists, and higher game points. But it also can give players the perception that a curved stick makes them more talented. Ultimately, the skill and talent you possess doesn't depend on the degree of your curve, but on the respect you have for your abilities.

TRIVIA FACT

Stan Mikita was a forerunner in another aspect of the game. When his ear was clipped by a puck, he fashioned a helmet that he wore for the rest of his career—a decade prior to the practice becoming a regulation in the NHL.

CHAPTER 2

WAYNE GRETZKY —
A TALE OF PRIDE AFTER THE TRADE

*"He changed the game in California and really, across
the United States. When Wayne came to LA, it put hockey on the
map in a whole new way."*

— Luc Robitaille on Wayne Gretzky's impact
with the LA Kings

January 26th, 1961 was a magnificent day for the world of hockey, as it was the day that "The Great One," Wayne Gretzky, was born in Brantford, Ontario, Canada. Walter Gretzky bought a house with a yard flat enough to build an ice rink every winter, where he taught his children to play a game he loved. A two-year-old Wayne was given a souvenir stick and taught stick skills; these skills—including shooting and skating—were honed with hours of practice on the backyard rink, with drills around bleach bottles and tin cans, and flipping pucks over scattered hockey sticks. Walter Gretzky had taught his children to pre-empt the puck's movement and to skate in that direction.

These tactics helped Wayne, as the youngest player to represent Canada in the 1977 Junior World Cup, to gain the title of the leading goal scorer. He firmly wrote his name in the pages of the junior greats by scoring 378 goals in the final season of the minor league. With the 1977-78 season, Wayne was contracted with the Indianapolis Racers, but was sold to the Edmonton Oilers the same season. During the time Wayne was with the Oilers, he was made captain and won the Stanley Cup for four seasons, namely 1983-84, 1984-85, 1986-87, and 1987-88.

While hockey remains a physical game, Wayne instilled grace and speed into his techniques, revolutionizing the way hockey is played. He was awarded the Art Ross Memorial Trophy for being the lead goal scorer in the NHL for 7 consecutive years from 1980 to 1987, and then again in 1989-90, 1990-91, and 1993-94. He also proceeded to win the title of the most valuable player of the year from the 1979-80 season to the 1986-87 season, being awarded the Hart Memorial Trophy again in the 1988-89 season.

THE TRADE-OFF

Feeling that he was settled with the Oilers, Wayne felt he had reached his groove, setting as many records as he was breaking, and gaining respect and acknowledgment from the hockey universe. Yet, shock reverberated among the hockey community when Wayne Gretzky and two of his teammates, Marty McSorley and Mike Krushelnyski, were traded to the Los Angeles Kings after the 1987-88 season.

Wayne heard the news of his transfer from his father, hours after the euphoria of winning the Stanley Cup for the Oilers. Negotiations had been in the works for a long while as the owner of the Oilers, Peter Pocklington, was experiencing financial challenges at the time. Wayne agreed to the transfer only if the Kings would take his teammates as well. The Kings traded them for Jimmy Carson and Martin Gélinas, as well as $15 million in cash and several first-round draft picks despite the head coach's protests. Canadians were so unhappy with the trade that the newly elected House leader of the New Democratic Party, Nelson Riis, tried to get the government to intervene.

A NEW HOMETOWN

Wayne didn't allow the change to stop him from doing what he did best—revolutionize the game of hockey! Appointed as the alternate captain, Wayne led the Kings past the Edmonton Oilers to finish in the playoffs against the Calgary Flames; however, they ultimately lost to the Flames, who won their first Stanley Cup that year. He once again helped the Kings to the Stanley Cup playoffs, reaching the second round, but losing to the Edmonton Oilers. The Oilers ultimately won the Stanley Cup and their new captain dedicated the win to his predecessor.

The LA Kings had one major rival—the LA Lakers—and when Brian McNall bought the team, he took the risk that bringing Gretzky to LA would increase interest in ice hockey. That risk paid off. Having Wayne appear in the team's newly revamped theme uniform of black and silver had the crowd streaming into the arena, and the Kings becoming a household name in Southern California.

The Grand Western Forum was sold out for the season, filling the seats after Wayne took up residence. This new interest from the fans also brought the spotlight on Wayne's new teammates: Bernie Nicholls and Luc Robitaille. Partnering with Wayne on the frontline, Bernie had one of the best seasons of his career, scoring 70 goals, 80 assists, and 150 points. This pushed the Kings to the Stanley Cup playoffs with the stats of 42-31-7, and changed the perception of the Kings being a NHL dry-spot to a springboard for future starts and free agents.

This opened the door for other teams in the southern California area, with the San Jose Sharks joining the NHL in the 1991-92 season, as well as the Anaheim Mighty Ducks in 1993. The Golden State became a permanent feature on the NHL roster. Many players who are born in the state of California have gone on to have standout careers in the NHL, and they include Jason Zucker, Thatcher Demko, and Auston Matthews (although he was raised in Arizona). These players were heavily influenced by the great one's legacy and, like Wayne, inspired more California-born players to find greatness.

The effects of Wayne moving to Los Angeles had more impact than just on the Kings. With Wayne's influence, the NHL could expand the game of hockey in parts of America that weren't traditionally hockey supporters. There were five more teams added by the mid-90s, including four American teams: Tampa Bay Lightning in 1992-92 and the Florida Panthers in 1993-94 in Florida, and the San Jose Sharks in 1991-92 and the Mighty Ducks of Anaheim in 1993-94 in California. The Kings and Ducks are among five U.S. teams who have gone on to win the Stanley Cup.

This was because the preseason tours would be directed at cities that didn't have a home team, encouraging more players to join the sport and creating a market for the NHL to establish teams in the new cities.

Before 1988, only five players had originated out of California; the number increased to 27 by 2013, including great players such as Jonathan Blum, Beau Bennett, and Emerson Etem. The one way that we can see how Wayne influenced hockey in California was by the fact that the number of players increased from 4483 in 1990-91 to an astounding 20,204 during the 2009-10 season. Many of them had grown up watching Wayne Gretzky shape the world of hockey and wanting to be like him.

TRIVIA FACT

Wayne's jersey number, 99, is the only number retired throughout the league, prohibiting any other player from wearing the number.

CHAPTER 3

MARK MESSIER — LEADING FROM THE FRONT

"My biggest fear is to stop being fearless. "

— Mark Messier

When Mark Messier was asked what his biggest fear was, he responded that he had no fears. And when we look at this prolific captain's career success, he truly showed neither fear nor doubt in his teams' abilities to beat the challenges set before them. Let's meet the man who won the Stanley Cup *six* times in his career.

Mark Messier was born on January 18, 1961, in Edmonton, Alberta, Canada. He had the advantage of having a professional hockey player as a father, who was also his first coach, as well as his lifelong hero. With his father's steady guidance and some friendly competition from his older brother Paul, Mark became a force to be reckoned with on the ice at a young age.

As an 11-year-old, Mark assisted the Spruce Grove Mets (whom his dad coached) as a stick boy. Spending hours at the rink allowed Mark the opportunity to sharpen his own skills, giving him an early entry into the Alberta Junior Hockey League (AJHL) at age 15, a league where the entry age was normally 16–20. For the next two years, Mark played 111 games and gained 140 points, achieving the position of captain by the time he was 17.

In the 1978-79 season, the Indianapolis Racers were looking for someone to replace Wayne Gretzky after his move to the Edmonton Oilers. Mark hesitated and, instead, signed a five-game amateur try-out, alternating between the Racers and the Mets, newly named the Saints after their move to St. Albert. After his five games, the racers presented Messier with a contract, but he declined and signed with the Cincinnati Stingers of the World Hockey Association (WHA) instead. It proved a good decision as the Racers declared bankruptcy a few weeks later.

His season with the Stingers wasn't as great as he had expected, resulting in only one goal in the 47 games he played. His skills were noticed by the Edmonton Oilers head coach, Glen Sather, who happily drafted Mark during the 1979 NHL draft. This allowed Mark to enter the NHL in his home province after the Oilers were merged into the NHL after the WHA dissolved. It was also the beginning of his 20-year partnership with Wayne Gretzky.

With Wayne as his partner, the masterful Mark pulled the Oilers to the playoffs, with Mark scoring 21 goals and 21 assists, accumulating 33 points in the regular season. Even though they lost to the Philadelphia Flyers, Mark grew in confidence and inspired his team to the next season's playoffs as well. His 23 goals and 43 points again helped the Oilers to the 1980-81 Stanley Cup quarter-finals, but the New York Rangers thwarted them. During the 1981-82 season, Mark and the Oilers were working their way to the top, especially with Mark's invitation to the All-Star game, and the team moving to the division semi-finals, but were once again disappointed as the LA Kings overthrew them.

THE MOOSE COMES TO LIFE

Besides being 6'2" and more than 200 pounds, Mark fearlessly faced opponents with his elbows, breaking one rival's cheekbone which gained him a 10-match suspension from scoring goals or assisting his teammates to score. Yet, it was not a strange sight to see him encouraging one of his teammates. With his violent streak, Mark had tenacity and determination, not afraid to push his team forward—whether it was with scoring goals, physical violence, or a kind word to his teammates. He earned the nickname "the moose."

His partnership with Wayne saw Mark score 101 points and led the Oilers to knock the New York Islanders off their four-time Stanley Cup pedestal to win the coveted trophy in the 1983-84 season. This opened the Stanley Cup floodgates for the Oilers as they won the 1984-85 finals, and then they took the cup again in the 1986-87 season, with Mark scoring 107 points.

Mark continued to dominate the ice with 111 points and his 6th All-Star participation, proceeding to lead the Oilers to their fourth Stanley Cup win, denying the Boston Bruins victory in 4 games.

WE'LL WIN TONIGHT

The 1993-94 season saw Mark leading the New York Rangers, his prowess on the ice was undisputed. The NYR finished in the playoffs against the New Jersey Devils, but not very successfully as they trailed three games to two. Mark shocked the world when he declared at a pregame press conference that the Rangers were going to win Game 6 and force a Game 7. The confidence with which he said it made the NHL universe think that he had some kind of magic hidden in his stick. The intention had been to instill some of that confidence into the team, not thinking that the other team would read the headline, and consequently react.

The Devils were ahead in goals, having scored two to the Rangers one at the end of the second period. The mood on the NYR bench was low as they watched the minutes tick down. And then came the third period.

Mark tied the game at 2-2 with his first goal, bringing the arena to their feet as they celebrated the goal. The celebration of his second goal was even more deafening, and the magic everyone had suspected him of seemed to be true. Just to ensure that the win was in the pocket, Mark shot the puck across center ice to score an empty-netter, making sure that the Rangers got their Game 7 to win the Stanley Cup.

The press statement was meant to encourage his team, show them how much he believed in them, and that he believed that they could win. It was the confidence with which Mark navigated his own game as well as his life. It was the confidence with which he took on any challenge, believing that he would overcome it. And overcome they did.

THE TROPHIES KEEP COMING

Trophies are significant emblems of a player's career, showing the growth and maintenance of their skills, sportsmanship, and leadership qualities. Trophies are not just to symbolize the team winning a major campaign or competition; they symbolize the team and the players overcoming challenges, injuries, trades, media attention, fan expectations, and personal intrigues. It is a visual representation of the dedication, commitment, and passion that a player puts into his craft, and the effort that he or she has made to develop within the game.

And if ever there was a man who needed a warehouse to display his career emblems, it is Mark Messier. If we had to list *every* award this giant of a man won throughout his career since the age of 15, we'd need to create volumes with several editions—but we will highlight those that embodied his motivation to never lose his fearlessness.

Besides holding the title of the youngest player in the AJH League, Mark has been achieving one—or two, or five—awards every season since 1979. During the 1,756 games he had played, scoring 694 goals and making 1,193 assists that gave him a total of 1887 points, Mark had also accumulated six Stanley Cup Trophies, two Ted Lindsay cups—formerly known as the Lester B. Pearson Cup for the most valuable player jointly elected by the NHL Players' Association, the Conn Smythe Trophy for being the most valuable player during the playoffs, and he won the Hart Trophy twice for the most valuable player in the league.

Mark also ended his career with several records, one of which was that he was the third highest points scorer in the regular season with 1,887 points, behind Wayne Gretzky and Jaromir Jagr. He was inducted into the WHA Hall of Fame in 2007, and the Canadian Sports Hall of Fame in 2009. He was named an Officer of the Order of Canada, honoring Mark Messier for his contribution to hockey and the exemplary role he played as a captain and an inspiration to later generations to play the game.

The highest honor that could be given to Mark, embodying the values he brought to hockey, was bestowed in 2006 when the NHL established the Mark Messier Trophy, which is awarded to players every month for the leadership quality they display on the ice. His two long-standing teams, the Edmonton Oilers and the New York Rangers, retired the number 11 after Mark stepped off the ice.

TRIVIA FACT

Mark's response of placing more value on humanity than the hard skills everyone associates with hockey to the question, "What talent would you most like to have?" shows the great person he is. Mark maintained that having compassion and empathy were the best qualities because they made you a better leader, understanding those around you with more compassion and empathy, and creating access and opportunity for those who are not in the same position as you. And when asked what his greatest triumph was, the humble Messier answered that it was his good fortune of being able to play with and against the best of the best of hockey players.

It was his resounding exclamation after game 5 of the 1994 playoffs that Messier was known for when he knowingly declared, "We're going to go in there and win Game 6".

CHAPTER 4

GORDON HOWE —
THE LEGENDARY MR. HOCKEY

"All hockey players are bilingual. They know English and profanity."
— Gordie Howe

He played 25 consecutive seasons for one team, retired, and then played in a different league for a few seasons before returning to the NHL when his team changed leagues and ultimately retired for a second and last time. He was invited to play in 23 All-Star games. He has several awards for top point scorer and most valuable player, scored 23 goals *per season* for 22 consecutive seasons, held the record for the most games played in a regular season, has four Stanley Cups under his belt, and has a unique hockey accolade named after him. He is a man who has buildings, bridges, and arenas named after him and the man who was nicknamed "Mr. Hockey." Who is this paragon?.

It is none other than legend maker Gordon "Gordie" Howe.

One of nine children, Gordie was born to a mechanic and construction worker father and stay-at-home mother on March 31, 1928, in Floral, Saskatchewan, Canada. When he was five, he suffered from a calcium deficiency because of the family's dire financial state, and this led to a strict exercise regime that would help him through some challenging times in his career.

His mother paid their neighbor $1.50 for a sack of odd things, and in it was a pair of ice skates for the four-year-old Gordie. Wearing several pairs of socks to make them fit, Gordie played ice hockey with the neighborhood children on the frozen surfaces. With immense creativity, Gordie tied blades to his shoes when he outgrew his skates. Hockey became his haven when he was teased as a child or faced academic challenges.

Despite not making it the first time he tried out for his school hockey team, Gordie was part of the team when the King George Community School won the league in 1941, 1942, and 1944. Because of his dedicated training regime, which included pucks in winter and tennis balls in summer, his performance caught the eye of a scout from the New York Rangers, who then invited Gordie to their training camp in Winnipeg—an event that Gordie found very overwhelming at 15.

THE MAKING OF MR. HOCKEY

His form was once again noticed by a leading team, and a scout for the Ontario Red Wings encouraged Gordie to attend. He was offered a contract with the team after showing his talent at the camp. Though he was supposed to start the 1944-45 season while he finished his schooling, Gordie decided to leave school and started working at the local metal works. During the 1945-46 season, Gordie was signed to the Omaha Knights, where he scored 22 goals and had 26 assists in the 51 games he played. At 18, Gordie moved over to the Red Wings for the 1946-47 season to debut in the NHL. This was the start of a very long and impressive career for Gordie Howe.

Joining fellow name-makers Ted Lindsay and Sid Abel to make what the history gurus called "the Production Line," becoming the best offensive lines in the history of the game, they were unable to stop the Toronto Maple Leafs from beating the Red Wings in the NHL championships in both the 1947-48 and 1948-49 seasons. The next season saw the *Production Line* become a force to be reckoned with as they drove the Red Wings to victory over the New York Rangers in a 4-3 game championship, winning the title for the first time in seven years. Gordie missed the playoffs after colliding with the boards and suffering a broken nose and cheekbone, as well as a cut to his eyeball and a bleed on his brain. To everyone's surprise, Gordie was back on the ice for the 1951-52 season. This would be the first of many injuries that could've ended his career, but Gordie showed resilience and determination to persevere through the challenges.

His precision was even more dangerous after his return from injury, as he not only went on to win the Stanley Cup but also won the Art Ross and Hart Memorial Trophies. He proceeded to add the latter to his collection in 1952-53, 1956-57, 1957-58, 1959-60, and 1962-63. With brutal grace, Gordie helped his team win the Stanley Cup in 1953-54 and 1954-55 against the Montreal Canadiens, cementing a rivalry between the two teams, as well as between Gordie and the Canadiens' star player, Maurice Richard. To the disappointment of many fans, that would be the last time the Stanley Cup graced the Detroit Red Wings with its presence during Gordie's residence.

The *production line* was disrupted when Ted Lindsay was traded to the Chicago Blackhawks in 1957 because he spoke out against the management and roused players into starting a players' union. At the time, Gordie stayed distant from the politics of the game and remained loyal to the team, though he disagreed with the management. He proceeded to do what he did best: create plays on the ice that would pave his way into the record books for years to come. November 10th, 1963 saw Gordie scoring his 545th goal against their biggest rivals, the Canadiens. This total climbed to 801 goals in the 1,767 NHL games he played in his 26-season tenure with the Red Wings—a record broken by fellow Canadian Patrick Marleau in 2021 when he finished his career at the San Jose Sharks with 1,779 games played.

RETIREMENT... OR JUST A BREATHER?

Gordie announced his retirement after the 1970-71 season, a quarter-century after his debut in the NHL. Canada honored him with an Order of Canada in 1971 for his generosity, leadership, and contribution to hockey, earning him entry into the International Hockey Hall of Fame in 1972. He attempted to participate in the management aspects of the Red Wings but preferred the more active role of being a player than administration.

The 1973-74 season saw Gordie join the World Hockey Association (WHA) team, Houston Aeros, alongside his sons, Marty and Mark. In the 285 games that Gordie played for them, he scored 121 goals, made 248 assists, and accumulated 369 points before moving to the New England Whalers in the 1977-78 season. They became the Hartford Whalers when they merged with the NHL a season later. Gordie again showed that his age did not affect his efficiency when he scored 53 goals with 86 assists to gain 139 points before he moved again after the 1978-79 season. Joining the Hartford Whalers for a final season in the NHL circuit, Gordie played all 80 games and scored an impressive 15 goals with 26 assists and racking up 41 points, to become the oldest player in the league at 52.

Gordon Howe still holds the record for total career games played with 2,186 when combining his WHA and NHL career games, with 975 goals scored, 1,383 assists, and a total of 2,358 points, numbers that are still unbeaten.

In 1997, at the age of 69, Gordie donned the uniform of the Detroit Vipers for the International Hockey League (IHL) and took to the ice for less than a minute... and true to form, scored a goal.

GORDIE THE UNFORGETTABLE

Gordie and his wife, Colleen, were renowned for giving back to the hockey fraternity, and are credited with initiating the first American team into the Junior NHL with the Junior Detroit Red Wings. They also created the Howe Foundation and the Howe Center for Youth Hockey Development.

The one way Gordie Howe's name is memorialized is by being the inspiration for a young Wayne Gretzky, *the Greatest Player of All Time* (GOAT). Wayne's biggest ambition was to be as great as his hero, sending him on a journey that would see him break Gordie's points record in 1989. Wayne also explained that he wore the number 99 as a tribute to Gordie.

Gordie had the reputation of being fierce on the ice, and this is evidenced in the injuries he suffered throughout his career, never backing down from a challenge, and sacrificing his body to prevent the opposing team from scoring. His never-give-up attitude pushed his teams to achieve their best, despite the circumstances, and brought forth more heroes in the interim. He also demonstrated that skill was everlasting, if you wanted it to be, when he scored his final goal at nearly 70 years old. His driving force on the ice had many younger generation players taking notes, inspiring them to push themselves harder to enhance their skills.

Off the ice, Gordon Howe was a giant of a different sort. Filled with compassion and empathy, Gordie was a friend more than a teammate. He was a leader within his home, as well as his community, and exemplified his humble beginnings by giving children in similar circumstances the opportunity to play the game they love. He loved his fans and never forgot to show his appreciation for their support.

When Gordie died on June 10th, 2016, a two-day memorial service was held in Detroit. Though he had a majestic career, Godie was remembered as the man behind the stick rather than the athlete. What stood out from youngest son Murray's eulogy to his father was that Gordie had never forgotten where he came from. He treated everyone with respect and consideration; whether it was helping servers set up an event where he was the guest speaker, or speaking to the president of the United States, he could make people feel comfortable in his presence.

Murray remembered one particular incident that made his father a hero in his eyes. They had been in a restaurant when a fan had asked his father for an autograph. A woman who had witnessed the scene approached

Gordie and asked if he was someone famous. Gordie had replied that he used to babysit the man.

Not only an outstanding athlete, he was a man well worth his accolades— living life with grace, compassion, and humor.

TRIVIA FACT

The unique hockey accolade named after Gordie Howe's fearless approach to the game was the Gordie Howe Hat Trick (GHHT). This is awarded to the player who can score a goal, have an assist, and be involved in a fight in the same game.

The record holder for this award is the Vancouver Canucks head coach, Rick Tocchet, with 18 GHHTs. Of the 2023-24 roster, Milan Lucic of the Boston Bruins is the current leader with 3 GHHTs. The NHL Chief Disciplinarian, Brendan Shanahan, finished his career with 17 GHHTs. The irony was that Gordie Howe himself only had 2 GHHTs in his entire career.

CHAPTER 5

WILLIE O'REE — BREAKING BARRIERS OF RACE AND COLOR

*"We should never let obstacles get in the way or be
an excuse for not trying."*
— Willie O'Ree

William "Willie" Eldon O'Ree—born on October 15th, 1935—had a family history that rivaled his standout NHL career.

Willie's grandparents made the brave decision to flee slavery and make a better life for their family. This entailed using the Underground Railroad from the US to Canada, and settling in Fredericton, New Brunswick. Willie was the youngest of 13 children and found the joy of skating at the tender age of 3. This led to the first passage into ice hockey, and Willie joined his first organized club by the time he was 5 years old.

Though the O'Rees were one of only two black families in Fredericton, Willie never felt discriminated against when it came to his hockey. He never felt that he was advantaged, or disadvantaged, because of his color or demography. He was respected for the talent he possessed and was coached, judged, and selected for his skills as any of his peers were.

PASSION IS FIRED

He had the advantage of being coached by his older brother, Richard, who taught Willie the importance of body checking—a great advantage for Willie when he joined the Fredericton Falcons in the New Brunswick Amateur Hockey Association (NBAHA) at 15 years old.

By the 1951–52 season, Willie was part of the Fredericton Merchants, affiliated with the York County Hockey League. He quickly progressed to the Fredericton Capitals in the New Brunswick Senior League, allowing Willie to play in the senior ranks in the 1953–54 season. The Capitals competed in the Allan Cup where Willie scored seven goals in seven matches.

Willie moved to Quebec at the age of 19, joining the Frontenacs in the Quebec Junior Hockey League, where he gave an impressive performance of 27 goals, 17 assists, and 44 points in the 43 games he played.

In the season 1955–56, Willie was faced with a moral dilemma. During a match against the Kitchener Canucks, Willie was struck by a puck in the face, breaking his nose and cheekbone, which resulted in him losing 95% of the vision in his eye. Knowing that he wouldn't be allowed to play, according to the NHL bylaws, Willie kept his vision challenges a secret after two months of recovery. He accommodated his blindness by turning his head nearly 180 degrees from his position on the left wing.

CROSSING THE BOUNDARIES

The Quebec Aces was a forward-thinking team and believed in indiscriminate line-ups. They had key starters such as Herb Carnegie (1949–1953), who had 77 goals and 121 assists with 198 points and Stan Maxwell (1956–1959)—two strong black players. Carnegie never played in the professional leagues, although he was inducted into the Canada Sports Hall of Fame. Willie had the honor of playing with both of these strong leaders. In the three seasons he played from 1956–57 to 1958–59, he scored 22 goals, 12 assists, and 34 points in the first, 13 goals, 19 assists, and 22 points in the second, and 9 goals, 21 assists, and 30 points in the last.

The Aces came to an agreement with the NHL's Boston Bruins, giving them access to the Aces' talent pool. This was how Willie got the opportunity to play with the Bruins on January 18th, 1958, debuting in the NHL as the first black player in history. The Bruins won that match against the Canadiens. Playing merely two games that season with the Bruins, Willie returned to the Acers but was called up to the Bruins again for the 1960–61 season. This time he scored 4 goals, participated in 10 assists, and totaled 14 points—again making history by scoring the first goal by a Black player in the NHL on January 1st, 1961, contributing to a 3–2 win over the Canadiens.

This auspicious occasion was overlooked by most of the big media outlets, with a Canadian journalist remarking that Willie's reception was indifferent, with no applause or animosity. What the journalist didn't realize was that Willie was already a household name in Canada because of his time with the Aces

Willie moved to several teams in various leagues, finding his groove with the Los Angeles Blades when the head coach changed his position from the left wing to the weaker right wing in the 1964–65 season. He proceeded to record his personal best of 38 goals in that season.

THE NOT-SO-SHINY SIDE OF HOCKEY

Though Willie was an exceptional player, his games were overshadowed by some negative reception during his 1972–73 AHL season. During a game, fans tossed cotton balls on the ice, as well as a black cat. He was also exposed to racial comments from an opponent during a match with the Chicago Black Hawks; Willie received a slam from an opponent's stick and his teeth were knocked out. This resulted in a fight on the ice, emphasizing Willie's challenges to playing hockey in America.

OVERCOMING THE CHALLENGES

Willie continued to play professional hockey until he retired in 1979, maintaining that the most discrimination he experienced was in the US. He became the first diversity ambassador for the NHL in 1998, in the position of the Director of Youth Development. He used this opportunity to spread the message of inclusion. He taught more than 120,000 children to play hockey through his programs. A partner of Willie's had often said that he was very dedicated and passionate about eliminating discrimination in the NHL, starting with the youth across America, and made steps to ease the way for future black stars.

The Pittsburgh Penguins honored Willie during Black History Month (February), highlighting his contributions and linking it to the establishment of the Willie O'Ree Academy. The program is designed to bring mentoring and social connections, paired with hockey techniques, to optimize opportunities for black youth in the Pittsburgh area interested in hockey. The Penguins' Foundation wanted to pay tribute to his trailblazing, highlighting how he opened the door to the 43 black players in the NHL since he broke through the barrier in 1957.

We also need to remember that Willie worked hard to overcome a disability that might have prevented him from playing at all, never mind being an NHL barrier buster. This has made Willie a double inspiration because he could speak to the youth who felt marginalized not only in color but, also, because of impairments. Willie worked tirelessly to ensure that everyone felt included and that they were not overlooked because of the color of their skin or physical challenges, speaking to the youth about his own experiences and encouraging them to always keep an open mind. His legacy is extended beyond the game, with players incorporating those values into their lives.

Besides valuable players such as Seth Jones, the three Subban brothers (Malcolm, P.K., and Jordan), Evander Kane, and many others following in Willie's footsteps, he was also awarded the Lester Patrick Trophy in 2002–03 for the work he put into promoting diversity. He was also honored in both Canada and America, including the Order of Canada, for his dedication as a youth mentor and a pioneering hockey player in 2008.

This follows an Order of New Brunswick in 2005 for the outstanding work he put into the community of his starter team, an honor that amplified the induction into the New Brunswick Sports Hall of Fame in 1984. He was inducted into the Hockey Hall of Fame in 2018 and, two years later, the Canada Sports Hall of Fame—showing the influence Willie had on the game and the respect his fellow NHL members had for him. Willie was offered an olive branch from the U.S. Congress by offering him a Congressional Gold Medal for what he had accomplished within the hockey community in 2019.

The NHL has also shown its appreciation of Willie's contributions with the Willie O'Ree Community Hero Award, acknowledging those who have a positive impact on the community while using the values of hockey to enhance people's lives. It also honored Willie by having the players display a decal on their helmets showing a banner with the words *Celebrating Equality* from Martin Luther King, Jr. Day from January 16th to the end of February 28th.

On the 64th anniversary of Willie O'Ree debuting for the Boston Bruins in the NHL, his number 22 was retired in 2022.

TRIVIA FACT

P.K. Subban, defenseman for the New Jersey Devils, was an example for the younger Jordan Subban—not only as a hockey teacher and coach but also as a young black man drafted into the NHL—who showed him what he could achieve. Meeting Willie O'Ree was a dream come true for

Jordan, who admired Willie for breaking through the barriers and opening doors for players of color, where conversations became more honest than in the days when Willie started. The message he learned from his hero was to just keep moving forward.

CHAPTER 6

VIKTOR TIKHONOV — A SOVIET GENERAL ON THE ICE

"The hardest thing is to teach a player to think on the ice.
That's what makes a good player."

— Viktor Tikhonov

From all accounts, reports, articles, player feedback, and general knowledge, Viktor Tikhonov was an authoritarian dictator. He controlled his players on the ice and off it. He drained them physically and mentally, drilling them for precision and accuracy, and shaping them into indomitable forces that ruled the World Championships, as well as the Olympics, for many years. He inspired fear into and demanded respect from everyone in the arena—whether it was a player, coach, or fan.

This formidable presence was only tarnished once, during the 1980 Olympic Games, when an insignificant mistake became memorable and put a stain on this remarkable coach's record. The cheeky victory of the American team was termed "the Miracle on Ice" because it highlighted the chink in the Russian armor—a gap that a hockey extraordinaire such as Tikhonov quickly strengthened.

Viktor Tikhonov was born on June 4, 1930, in what was the USSR. Viktor played for VVS Moskva, a team of the Soviet Air Forces, when he turned 19. From the 1948-49 season till the 1962-63 season, Viktor divided his playing time between the VVS and Dynamo Moscow. He appeared in 296 games, scoring 35 goals. With each of the teams, he won several gold medals, 3 Russian National Championships with VVS, and one with Dynamo. In 1952, he won the USSR Cup with VVS.

COACH OR GENERAL?

He displayed exceptional discipline on the ice, focusing on precision and puck control. He carried this discipline into his coaching, where some players have described him as being as regimented as an army general. His drills were ferocious, and he pushed his players on and off the ice. He believed that speed and skill needed to be a part of the player's muscle memory—something that is instinctual rather than a conscious movement. It's a distinction that can lose a team seconds on the ice.

He achieved this strict discipline by isolating his teams from their families and having them stay in barracks for months at a time. He would combine this with workouts four times a day, having players drag tractor tires as they skated. He employed tactics that were close to torture techniques used by enemy armies. The players were also no strangers to getting as little sleep as was humanly possible during the training camps or just before a game. As controversial as it was, Viktor believed that the lack of sleep would give the players focus, as well as perseverance, in long games.

Viktor had been relentless during off-ice training, using methods that weren't what would be considered orthodox. These drills might include using equipment such as weighted vests or other equipment to practice their shots. He hoped this would make the player more adaptable in true game scenarios. This was often paired with small-group competitions, giving the players free rein to play as hard as possible, and encouraging his players to be able to perform at their best, no matter the circumstances. Viktor also made sure that he kept his players on a strict diet, including controlling the portion sizes and restricting certain food choices for the team; he believed that it would enhance their performance while also ensuring that they remained in peak physical condition.

THE INDOMITABLE FORCE

The Soviet team, under Viktor's leadership, was a force that few teams could overcome. The team was well-versed in quick, sharp, and accurate passes; this led to fast and hard goals. Their defenses weren't as aggressive as their American counterparts, but no less effective, keeping the puck in the opposing team's half more than what they needed to defend their own net.

During the 1954 World Championships, the Soviet team took the gold medal in their debut tournament, defeating the (then) world power, Canada. Though they had an impeccable record in the international ice hockey arena, they excelled under Viktor Tikhonov when he took over in 1977 and led the Red Army to the top of the podium in the 1979 World Championships.

Despite the great loss in the 1980 Olympic games against the Americans and having to settle for the silver medal, the Soviet team became a forceful presence on the ice and dominated most of the tournaments in which they competed. They had the added advantage of maintaining their core team, unlike the Canadian and American teams who had to construct new teams with nearly every competition because their NHL-signed players weren't allowed to compete in the international spectrum.

The loss only spurred them on to win gold in the 1984 and 1988 Olympics, as well as the 1992 Games with the newly reformed team after the dissolution of the U.S.S.R. Between the Olympics, Viktor led the team to eight world championships.

On a national level, CSKA Moscow won 14 national championships under Viktor's leadership. He showed his mettle as a coach, presenting results from game to game and tournament to tournament, whether on a local or international level.

Viktor wasn't too enthusiastic about his players wanting to go overseas, especially to exhibit their skills in the NHL, either in America or Canada. Players had reported that Viktor released them if he had any inkling that they were interested. It was after the 1980 Olympics that many of them rebelled against his authoritarian coaching techniques, fought for their freedom, and followed their dreams to America.

TRIVIA FACT

Viktor Tikhonov was such a prolific coach that his son—Viktor "Vasily" Tikhonov, Jr.—had also played under his coaching, but then moved to the NHL where he finished his career as a coach with the San Jose Sharks before he sadly passed away.

His grandson, also named Viktor Tikhonov (III), played with the Phoenix Coyotes in the NHL before moving on to SKA St. Petersburg in the Kontinental Hockey League. Tatjana "Tiki" Tikhonov has also shown her grandfather's influence in her life by playing for local clubs in Russia before moving into coaching roles around the world, including the San Jose Sharks AAA team. Tatjana currently has her own ice hockey academy that helps current NHL players improve their skills.

CHAPTER 7

BOBBY ORR — KNOWN FOR HIS ICONIC GOAL

"The biggest thing I have learned is you can't fight fate.
Life is short and you have to make the most of it."

— Bobby Orr

One would think that being the goaltender on the team is the most important job, but we need to argue this point. Goaltenders are vital, and we won't diminish their role on the team and how agile these players are. But we need to pay attention to our defensemen—special attention.

Defensemen are notoriously heavy-handed in their play, putting their bodies and careers on the line to protect their goaltenders. In the early years of hockey, defensemen were positioned on the wings and weren't afraid to lose their teeth, break noses, or even spend a few days in the hospital to stop an opponent from scoring. Defensemen were predominantly large and speed was not a necessity for their resume. In the past few years, this position was revolutionized, requiring the position to be more versatile and fluid—above and beyond just defending their halves. And there is one man who made sure that the defensemen had more of the ice than ever before: Bobby Orr.

Robert "Bobby" Orr, born March 20th, 1948 in Parry Sound, Ontario, not only used his body to fulfill his role but also took the initiative and crossed the ice to create an offensive defenseman. This meant that he took an active role in scoring goals, steering the puck to the opponents' half to set up assists for his forwards with exacting accuracy. Bobby never took a back seat to create opportunities, whether it was for his teammates to score or for his own shot to hit the back of the net. He exemplified the dual positions of protector-defender and producer. Bobby was able to combine four components that are now a career necessity for any defenseman—toughness, speed, skill, and grace.

Bobby started his skating career at the age of 4; at age 12, was marked as a potential player for the professional leagues because of his size and ability. He caught the eye of the Boston Bruins scouts during the Parry Sound Bantam All-Star Tournament. It took 58 minutes of play for him to make an impression on the scouts, even while he spent 2 minutes in the penalty box. At 14, Bobby signed a contract with the Bruins, commuting to games to play against 19- and 20-year-olds. By the time Bobby turned 16, he was already being considered better than Gordie Howe. At 18, Bobby signed on for two years with the Bruins, the biggest contract to be signed by a rookie.

Despite an injury he suffered during the summer before the 1967-68 season, Bobby was named Rookie of the Year. During the 1969-70 season, Bobby won the Art Ross for scoring, Hart for most valuable player (MVP), Norris for best defenseman who used their all-round abilities, and the Conn Smythe (MVP of the playoffs)Trophies—a first for any player to achieve in one season. At the time, the 87 assists and 120 points he had earned were the highest for a defenseman.

Bobby showed a fierceness on the ice that was hard to match, outskating many of the forwards in the rink with finesse and grace. Being the youngest player on the ice didn't intimidate him, and his confidence allowed him to make the plays he did—not only ending the season with the most assists for a defenseman, but also keeping the other team on their toes and never knowing what to expect from him. This confidence led him to win 8 consecutive James Norris Trophies in his career. This does not diminish the 3 Hart Trophies, 2 Art Ross Trophies, a Calder Award, 2 Conn Smythe Trophies, a Lester Patrick Trophy, a Ted Lindsay Award, or the 2 Stanley Cups he had lifted with the Boston Bruins.

As a defenseman, Bobby placed his body in harm's way numerous times during the game. And though he was at the peak of his physical fitness, he was afflicted by injuries that kept him sidelined for months at a time, keeping him from the ice. Despite this, he continued winning awards that showed his quality as a sportsman and a team leader, though he never wore the captain's "C." In 1974-75, Bobby had his best season as he scored 46 goals with 135 points, cutting his career short at the age of 27; he still played 10 games in the 1975-76 season for the Bruins, as well as 26 games for the Chicago Blackhawks as a free agent.

The imagination grapples to understand what more Bobby could have achieved if he hadn't needed to endure several knee operations. When he played his final game on November 8th, 1978, Bobby retired with an average of 1.4 points per game. This means that Bobby scored 270 goals and 951 points in the 657 career games he had played.

Bobby Orr was a player who influenced many others with his insistence that a defenseman should be more than a heavy shoulder behind the blue line. He combined savvy stick work with agility and speed, contradicting whatever perceptions were held about large defenders. He gave other defensemen some competition with records to beat and maneuvers to improve. He changed the way hockey was played in more ways than just the defenseman's role; he also changed the way centers needed to negotiate the puck to the net and how goaltenders defend their halves.

Bobby Orr's name is memorialized on many trophies, buildings, foundations, and media sources. You cannot be a fan of hockey in any country without knowing the impact that Bobby had on the game. The influence he generated gave the impression that he was part of the NHL family for decades (remembering Gordie Howe) rather than the 11 seasons he roared onto the ice—first for the Boston Bruins, and then the Chicago Blackhawks. There is one thing that will have Bobby Orr forever impressed in the minds of the hockey universe.

FLYING INTO IMMORTALITY

The Bruins were dominating the 1969-70 season, and Bobby had the season of his career with 33 goals and 87 assists in 76 games. He was awarded the Hart, Norris, Art Ross, and Conn Smythe Trophies. By the last of the playoff games, Bobby barely trailed behind Phil Esposito who had 13 goals and 14 assists. The Stanley Cup finals extended into a 4 game bonanza, the Bruins overpowering the St. Louis Blues with large goal differences. Game 4, played on May 10th, 1970, saw both teams finish with 3 goals each, leading the match into overtime, after 3 periods of tense interaction between both teams.

The 40 seconds of overtime seemed like an eternity when the Blues lost the puck for Bobby to reap it up. This helped Wayne Carleton to shoot the puck to the point, before Don Awrey took up the play, sliding the puck to the net. Glenn Hall blocked the shot with ease. The ricochet was redirected by Derek Sanderson back to the net but missed, and the teams fought to get possession again before Sanderson tried to net the puck again.

The crowd in the Boston Gardens went wild when Bobby reached for the puck with his skate before shifting it onto his stick, passing two opponents, and passing it back to Sanderson. He sent the puck back to Bobby as he went across the net, and Bobby sent the puck beyond Glenn Hall, the goaltender for the St. Louis Blues, for the Bruins to win the cup.

In the follow-through of the shot, Blues defenseman Noel Picard hooked Bobby's skate and tripped the prolific defenseman in the same instance Bobby jumped in celebration and the infamous picture of Bobby "flying" was captured by Ray Lussier, a photographer with the Boston *Record*

American newspaper. Celebrations were well-warranted as it was the first win for the Bruins since 1941.

Considering that Bobby Orr was all of 22 when the image was captured, what he achieved was embodied in it, cementing his Superman status. He showed that age is something that can't hold you back. It shouldn't hinder you from making your mark on the game, taking ownership of your skills, and ensuring that you become a force to be reckoned with. Bobby used everything he had to his advantage—his age, size, speed, and, most importantly, his varied skills as a talented defenseman.

TRIVIA FACT

There is a statue of Bobby's flying moment outside of Boston's TD Gardens. It is 800 pounds of bronze, designed by Harry Weber and revealed to the public on May 10th, 2010—30 years after that iconic goal. During the COVID-19 pandemic, the statue was dressed in Boston Bruins Hospital scrubs, a visual reminder to be cautious.

CHAPTER 8

JAROMIR JAGR'S
DRAFT DAY DECEPTION

"I want to be the best player in the world,
and I want to win the Stanley Cup."

— Jaromir Jagr

Many could say that Jaromir Jagr is a deceptive man. At 6 ft 3 in. and 230 lb, Jaromir could still outskate rookies with yards to spare. This does not mean that he was faster on his skates only, but he was faster in puck control, shooting, and scoring. He was able to fake slap shots, direction, and maneuvers to cover space as quickly as possible. He could feign moves around the opposing teams to make amazing goals and creative assists.

Other parts of his career could be called questionable, though this had not stopped him from being one of the top scorers in NHL history. Instead, it made the management, fans, and critics pay attention. His methods are almost forgotten when you look at his work ethic, even at the age of 52, while he still plays for his local club. Besides doing 1,000 squats a day, he also uses a 25 lb stick to practice with, while wearing a weighted vest and ankle weights. He also practices his shots with 6 in. go-kart tires and uses water to increase the resistance for his stickhandling abilities.

Born in Kladno, Czech Republic, on February 15th, 1972, Jaromir had played for his country since he was 15 years old. Jaromir was a boundary breaker since the beginning of his career, being the first player to get his government's acceptance to play in the NHL. He was scouted by several teams before being drafted by the Pittsburgh Penguins in 1990.

CAREER PROGRESS

Jaromir Jagr is one name known throughout the whole NHL universe, synonymous with movement, goals, and success. In the 1,733 games that Jaromir had played in his career, he had scored 766 goals with an impressive 1,155 assists, and 1921 points, second only to Wayne Gretzky.

Jaromir played for the Penguins from the 1990-91 to 2000-01 season, a total of 806 games with 439 goals and 640 assists, scoring 1079 points. The Penguins won two Stanley Cups during Jaromir's first two seasons, and he also won the Art Ross Trophy five times, as well as the Hart Trophy once during his stint with them. This is in addition to winning the Ted Lindsay Award in the 1998-99, 1999-00, and 2005-06 seasons.

He was then traded to the Washington Capitals in the 2001-02 season, and he went on to show his merit as a graceful player, even if his stats declined a bit, making the All-Star team again. When he was traded to the New York Rangers during the 2003-04 season, it seemed to be the change Jaromir needed because, in his 2005-06 season, he scored 54 goals and 69 assists, totaling 123 points setting him at second place in the league. Though he only spent 3 seasons with the Rangers, Jaromir had a positive impact on the team because they made the playoffs in all of those seasons.

Jaromir then joined the Continental Hockey League in Russia for three seasons when he became a free agent in 2007-08, before returning to the NHL to play for the Philadelphia Flyers in 2011. For the next few seasons, Jaromir moved between teams, from the Dallas Stars and Boston Bruins with one season each, and the New Jersey Devils for two before settling at the Florida Panthers for three seasons. He narrowly missed out on the Stanley Cup with the Bruins, but hit another record—the most years between finals appearances with 21 years. The Panthers had allowed him to accumulate 1,888 points, second only to "The Great One": Gretzky.

He only played 22 games with the Calgary Flames because of some injury concerns. He returned to the Czech Republic and his home team, Kladno Hockey Club. This is not the first time he has returned to his home country, participating in various tournaments, and earning several trophies—gold in the 1998 Olympic Games, bronze in the 2006 Olympics—as well as participating in the Winter Games in Vancouver in 2010 and Sochi in 2014.

THE GREAT DECEPTION

With the 1990 draft, Jaromir Jagr was a player wanted by several teams, including the Quebec Nordiques, the Vancouver Canucks, the Detroit Red Wings, and the Philadelphia Flyers. Jaromir took his time, delaying his commitment to them. Some would argue that by doing this, he was increasing his desirability and creating a bidding war among the climbs. Some rumors were that Jaromir had told the Canadian teams that he wasn't eager to leave his home in the Czech Republic at the young age of 18, while another says that he told them that he wasn't prepared to join the NHL yet Others claimed that he was seeking attention. This meant that, though they wanted Jaromir's skills in their rink, they passed him over during the 1990 draft picks.

This left him available for the team he wanted to play, and he was elated when the Penguins drafted him as the fifth pick in the first round. Though it surprised them, it would be years later when general manager, Craig Patrick, would have Jaromir's confession about what he had told the other teams when they interviewed him—something the Penguins were happy about at the time.

Mario Lemieux played a pivotal role in Jaromir's decision to go to Pittsburgh. His determination to share the ice with his hero had him turning down top teams, though they offered him the same specs that the Penguins did. The match was one made in heaven when Pittsburgh won the Stanley Cup in two consecutive seasons 1990-91 and 1991-92.

Jaromir used the opportunity to learn from his idol, speaking to him every moment he could, whether on or off the ice. Mario was able to guide Jaromir with his quiet skill, making them the most intimidating combination on the ice, bringing out the best of the younger Jaromir's career. Between their iconic stickhandling and puck control, the two of them amassed goals and assists that led them into the record books of NHL history. Their relationship was cemented by Jaromir emulating this strict work ethic and team mentality throughout his career. Jaromir was always sure to speak about Mario's support in the early days.

As the NHL world watched Jaromir Jagr's number 68 lift to the roof of the Penguins' home stadium, the chants of fans echoing around the rink as the iconic number is retired, there is no doubt that Jaromir Jagr will always have a home at Pittsburgh. Whether it was manipulation, whether it was a large-scale deception, or whether it was fate—Jaromir had made sure that one of his dreams came true: playing alongside his hero. Jagr's number was retired on February 18, 2024, 34 years after it debuted in the Penguins' colors, clearly showing that home can be what you make it. Just ask Jaromir.

TRIVIA FACT

At 52, Jaromir is the owner and player of Rytiri, the club he played for as a child, following in his father's footsteps to preserve the town of Kladno. He grew up on a farm that his grandfather, also Jaromir, owned. During World War II, the communist government confiscated a large portion of the farm, something Jaromir Sr. would accept willingly, and was subsequently imprisoned. A movement of the people wanting independence was overthrown by Warsaw Pact tanks in 1968, the same year that Jaromir Sr. died. So, to honor his grandfather, Jaromir wore number 68 throughout his NHL career.

CHAPTER 9

CONNOR BEDARD
CORNERED BAD BRUISES

"I just love being out on the ice, competing with my teammates, and striving to be better every single day. Hockey's not just a game to me; it's a way of life."

— Connor Bedard

This is the way a neighbor describes living next door to Connor Bedard, the newest superstar whose name has been echoing around the arenas of the NHL since his draft in 2023. This is a result of hours of shooting a puck into a net in the street, his foot skills sharpened on a pair of in-line skates, his stick skills exercised at all unusual hours of the day and night—rain or sunshine, in the backyard, in the street, and in the house—to his mother's chagrin as she watched her vases become victims to his practices.

Born in North Vancouver on July 14th, 2005, Connor started skating at the age of 3; it wasn't one of his favorite activities, though, until his older sister, Madisen, added a stick and a puck, and he was hooked. These tools became an extension of Connor, and he even went on vacation only if he was able to take his gear along.

Connor was unstoppable. He wouldn't let anything stand in the way of him playing; he would use what he could to his advantage, whether it was shooting hundreds of pucks into a net in the yard or a rink at the North Shore Winter Club during the off-season. His dedication and passion were finally directed to a minor league when he was 5. He joined the Western Hockey League and was a prolific goal-scorer for the Regina Pats. At 15, he was the first Western Hockey League (WHL) player to be awarded the exceptional player label. And like his namesake, Connor McDavid, he became one of only 9 players to be awarded the title in the Canadian Hockey League. It is no surprise, as Connor scored 12 goals in 15 games with 28 points during the WHL's shortened season of 2020-21. The next season witnessed Connor scoring 51 goals with 100 points in 62 games, giving him a prime position on Team Canada at the World Junior Hockey Championship.

Connor scored an average of at least 3 goals per game in the 2022 championship—the second 16-year-old Canadian to do so. The other was Wayne Gretzky in 1977. He also tied another record for the number of goals scored in a world junior game, this one with Mario Lemieux.

His work ethic was eventually rewarded when he became the first pick in the first round of the 2023 NHL draft, upholding the lessons he had learned from Matthew Barzal, a friend whom Connor sought to emulate. His former childhood teammate, Andrew Cristall, was impressed with Connor's drive, explaining that he could score twice as hard, twice as fast, and twice as long as any of the other players.

Connor Bedard is a rising star who doesn't seem to be burning out soon, holding his reputation as a first-class player high, igniting a fire in the younger fans of the NHL, and inspiring the next generation of players. He works hard, but this comes with a big risk of injury.

WHEN AN INJURY BECOMES A GOLDEN LESSON

Serious injuries are as much a part of ice hockey as blunt skates and breaking sticks. Some injuries allow you back on the ice a few days later; others could keep you out of the game for months. This happened to Connor when he was 12 and crashed against the boards, breaking his right wrist in such a way that it could have affected the way he used his arm for the rest of his life. Connor decided to follow the doctor's advice and rest his arm for the required 12 weeks, staying out of formalized hockey until he had the all-clear from his medical team. This didn't mean that Connor rested though.

Connor continued to work on his shots, foot skills, and puck control without his dominant hand coming into play. He practiced the grip of his top hand, strengthening and maximizing its capability until he could shoot the puck with as much control, speed, and power as he could with both hands.

The one thing everyone noticed was that when Connor returned to the ice, his stick skills had improved exponentially. The power in his top hand had effectively given him more control over his shots, making them more accurate and faster. It has also made him more dangerous on the puck as he could control it using either hand with equal force, making him unpredictable.

When he speaks about this adaptation, he explains that it was a matter of maintaining his routine and conditioning his body more than practicing. His thoughts had not been about strengthening his top hand but keeping himself in playing form the best way he could think of.

His dedication paid off. As mentioned, Connor became the first player in the WHL to achieve exceptional status, vaulting him into the major leagues at the age of 15. He scored 50 goals with 51 points in 62 games, making him the youngest player in the WHL to do so. He broke a record set in the 1995-96 season when he scored 71 goals, had 72 assists, and got 143 points in 57 games.

He also played his way onto a very prestigious list when he scored 36 points consisting of 17 goals and 19 assists on the international arena of the world junior championship games. He ranked fourth behind Pavel Bure who made 39 points in 21 games, Robert Reichel with 40 points in 21 games, and Peter Forsberg who scored 42 points in 14 games.

Connor continues to show his class with his on-going passion and hard work. Peers used words like incredible and exceptional to describe the rookie who was shattering long-standing records held by such greats as Mario Lemieux and Wayne Gretzky.

Connor Bedard is being compared to many of the stand-out players in the NHL because he used many of their techniques and made them his own, combining them into the special blend that was rocketing him into the hockey stratosphere. Besides sharing a name, Connor's career has also paralleled that of Connor McDavid, both in the junior leagues as well as being the first pick in the draft. The NHL Central Scouting director, Dan Marr equates Connor's speed to that of McDavid at the same age, mixed with a quiet calculation.

One of Connor's first coaches, Jon Calvano, had pointed out similarities between Alex Ovechkin's ability to get out of any situation with Auston Matthew's ability to make a shot without breaking his stride. Calvano had also been proud of Connor's ability to make his teammates look and feel good.

In his own way, Connor was a role model to another generation of players incorporating his techniques into their way of playing. He maintained an air of humility in his work, staying later to practice more stick skills and footwork, not taking his position among the greats for granted.

TRIVIA FACT

Jon Calvano recalled the time when the team manager of the Vancouver Vipers in the AAA program asked each of the 5-year-old players what number they wanted to be. He remembered that they had to have votes for the popular numbers 87 and 97, worn by Sidney Crosby of the Pittsburgh Penguins and Conner McDavid of the Edmonton Oilers respectively. And though Wayne Gretzky's 99 was yearned for but no one dared ask for it. Connor chose the next best number—98.

When he was asked who had that number, he confidently told them that he did. And he is making sure that it is becoming synonymous with his name, just as Wayne Gretzky made 99.

CHAPTER 10

THE DOMINATOR DOMINIK HASEK

"I will do anything to stop the puck, no matter how ridiculous it might look to someone else."

— Dominik Hasek

With speed, grace, agility, and reflexes that would put a ninja to shame, Dominik showed his dominance of a game in more than just his fearless presence. Dominik eviscerated records set by previous goaltenders, winning more than just the coveted Vezina Trophy, but also the Hart Trophy and several more in his career. This dominating presence started as a five-year-old who was eventually asked to play the position of goalie on a team of nine-year-olds. He was fearless.

WHERE IT STARTED

Born in old Czechoslovakia on January 29th, 1965, Dominic had worn a pair of modified skates, where the blades had been screwed into the bottom of his shoes to try out for his local team at the age of five. While waiting for his turn, he watched as the team of the nine-year-olds struggled without a goaltender. The tall-for-his-age Dominik agreed to join their team and hasn't looked back since. He was hooked on hockey!

Dominik worked hard to become immovable in the net, practicing for hours with his grandfather and stopping any projectile from passing him—whether it was a puck, a ball, or a rolled-up piece of paper. This determination to succeed paid off. He became the most limber goalie for his age, finding innovative ways to get to ice-level quickly. Being tall for his age was definitely to his advantage as he was able to cover his net without much strain. It was also the time he perfected his "fish-flop" move. Dominik could drop to the ice to stop a shot, as well as stick out his hands or legs to stop a rebound, making his net impenetrable. Dominik also used what was available to him to stop a puck, and would often use his body, blocking a puck with his blocker hand and without his stick.

Orthodox or not, Dominik was playing professionally for Pardubice Hockey Club in Czechoslovakia at 16, with no intentions of leaving his home country. Due to world politics at the time, when the Chicago Blackhawks drafted him in 1983, he hadn't even been aware that they were scouting him while he played for the national team.

Dominik continued to dominate in the Czech Republic, contributing to his team winning the championships in 1987 and 1989, as well as being voted the goaltender of the year from 1986 to 1990. He was awarded the title of the league's best player in the year in 1987, 1989, and 1990. Eight years after being drafted by the Chicago Blackhawks but forced to continue playing in his home country, Dominik finally made his way to Chicago and played second to Ed Belfour, while training under former Russian goaltender, Vladislav Tretiak, who was now the goalie coach for the Blackhawks.

His trade to the Buffalo Sabres in 1992 allowed Dominik to display his talents even more. He stood in for Grant Fuhr, who had a series of injuries in the 1993-94 season. This opened the eyes of his coaches, who realized that he was worthy as a starter goalie.

THE DOMINATOR RULES

Dominik got starting status and was never on the bench during face-off again. He had unbelievable game stats for that season, with a save percentage of .930, a goals-against-average of 1.95, and seven shutouts, an overall 30-20-6. This helped the Sabres into the playoffs against the New Jersey Devils and brought Dominik into the limelight.

Game 6 was the one that had catapulted Dominik into the pages of NHL history. New Jersey Devils was leading the playoffs 3-2 and was determined to take the Stanley Cup on the Sabres' home ground. The Sabres were determined to give the Devils a fight. The fans had to endure three full periods with no goals. The game ran into overtime, but when no goal was scored, it ran into another overtime, and then a third, the extra time on the ice taking its toll on the players, making them slower and less focused. Dominik could see the extended game affecting his teammates and he decided to stand strong in the net. This meant shutting out every one of the 70 shots that the Devils sent toward his crease, holding them off until the Sabres scored in the fourth overtime session, winning the match. Dominik the Dominator was crowned even if the Devils won Game 7 and took the Cup that season.

In the years that Dominik played for the Sabres, his dominance echoed across the seasons, pushing the team to be the strongest they had been in years. When Dominik wasn't making game stats on the ice, he was earning trophies. The 1993-94 season saw him winning the Vezina Trophy and sharing the William M. Jennings Trophy with Fuhr. He again won the Vezina Trophy the next season with his save percentage of .930, goal against average (GAA) of 2.11, and five shutouts.

Maintaining exceptional figures through the next few seasons, including first place in the Northeast Conference in the 1996-97 season, becoming an unstoppable presence in the Sabres' half. This gave Dominik his third Vezina Trophy as well as the Hart Memorial Trophy and then bestowed the Lester B. Pearson Award. The next season, Dominik showed his dominion over the ice and headed the NHL tables with 2149 shots against, 2002 saves, and a percentage of .932, gaining a career-high of 13 shutouts. In addition to the Hart Trophy and Pearson Award, Dominik once again lifted the Vezina Trophy for the fourth time. He was the first goaltender to win the Hart Trophy twice, showcasing his talents with confidence.

INTERNATIONAL DOMINANCE

The 1998 Winter Olympics in Japan was a game changer for the NHL players as it was the first time that they were allowed to participate. Dominik played for his home country, the rest of the world not holding much hope for the Czechoslovakian team, especially against the stronger American and Canadian teams. Dominik didn't allow that to intimidate them but decided to use it to his advantage. The team consisted of two well-known players, Jaromir Jagr and Dominik Hasek, but Dominik had confidence in the little-known Czech team.

Finland and Kazakhstan stood no chance against the Czechs, and everyone held their breath when they had to face the force of the Russian team, who had been sweeping gold in every Olympic competition since 1984. True to form, the Russians won 2-1, but this didn't stop the underdog Czech team from meeting America in the quarterfinals. Dominik led from his box, stopping a whopping 38 out of 39 goals from the Americans, and proceeded to win that match 4-1.

This win pushed Czechoslovakia into the semi-finals and again the world held its breath as the underdogs faced a Canadian team that consisted of 13 future Hall of Famers. The game was tied at one all at overtime, and a shootout ensued. The Canadians didn't seem to be playing with their regular aggression. Dominik showed why he was called the "Dominator" when he blocked the shots of Theo Fleury, Joe Nieuwendyk, and the incomparable Ray Bourque, while a fourth shot from Eric Lindros rebounded off the post. Everyone sat on the edge of their seats when Dominik blocked the shot from Brendan Shanahan.

Robert Reichel faced the Canadian goalie Patrick Roy, and scored on his first shot attempt, giving Czechoslovakia their 2-1 win.

They faced the Russians in the finals. The Czechs dominated the match, keeping the Russians in their own half of the rink for the majority of the game, scoring a goal and winning gold—bringing a lifelong dream of Dominik's to fruition. They were Olympic gold medalists. Once again, Dominik showed why he was the best goalie in the NHL, if not the world, as he finished the Olympics with a goals against average (GAA) of 0.97 and a save percentage of .961.

Enumerating Dominik Hasek's various awards and accomplishments will diminish the work and dedication that this amazing man has put toward perfecting his skill. He pushed through more challenges than most people would face in their careers, determined to become the best in the field—or on the ice as it was. What stands out about Dominik Hasek is that he strayed true to himself, adapting what he could improve and enhancing his talents to be strong in the net for his team and country.

DOMINIK HASEK, THE DOMINATOR

What people thought were his weaknesses, Dominik used to his advantage, using the feedback to work through the negatives and turn them into positives. One example of this was when Dominik played for the Chicago Blackhawks; he was able to tune out the praise that the media had for Ed Belfour because he couldn't understand English. This allowed him to focus on his own brand of tending without being influenced by Belfour's reputation.

One coach described Dominik's drop and block as a fish flopping around in front of the net. Again, besides keeping his blocking hand out of danger, Dominik didn't allow this to make him feel insecure. Instead, he used that as motivation to practice even more, becoming the most influential goaltender in the 1990s.

It appears that what makes Dominik the "Dominator" is not the many awards he won. It's not the many shutouts per season or goals that he saved. It wasn't the many wins he could take credit for, nor the way he filled a net to intimidate an opposing team. What truly makes Dominik the Dominator is the never-give-up spirit of the man. This was the man who wouldn't give up—the man who found courage in the face of adversity. *That* is what made Dominik Hasek indomitable.

TRIVIA FACT

Dominik had such an impact on the hockey world that he was not only inducted into the Hall of Fame on November 17, 2014, but he has also been inducted into the International Ice Hockey Hall of Fame, as well as the Czech Ice Hockey Hall of Fame.

CHAPTER 11

RAY BOURQUE —
A RAY OF HOPE AND RESILIENCE

"I always try to lead by example, whether it's on the ice or off.
Hard work and dedication are the keys to success."

— Ray Bourque

Raymond Jean Bourque was born in Montreal, Quebec on December 28, 1960. He grew up watching his home team, the Montreal Canadiens, during their epic run in the 1970s, drawing inspiration from their quick-paced offense and crushing defense. He drew the eyes of the bigger leagues from a young age when he played in the Quebec Major Junior Hockey League (QMJHL) at the age of 16, and was drafted in 1979 as the Boston Bruins' pick at 19. He proceeded to display the raw talent that they needed by scoring 65 points. This was a record he set as the most points accumulated by a defenseman in the NHL as a rookie. This not only earned him the Calder Trophy but, also, a spot on the NHL's first All-Star team. It was the first time that a player who wasn't a goalie had earned both in one season.

From the start, Ray was a force to be reckoned with, opening his goal account by scoring against the Winnipeg Jets in the first game of the season 1979-80, giving the Bruins players and fans some hope that their Stanley Cup drought had ended. This was not to be, yet, as the Bruins lost to the New York Islanders in the Quarterfinals despite Ray setting the ice on fire.

From the 1979-80 season to the 1982-83 season, Ray's extraordinary display on the ice gave the Bruins enough leadership to enter the postseason games, scoring an average of 60 points per season, except for the 1982-83 season where he scored 73 points. The need for the ultimate silver drove both the team and Ray to strive for perfection, each game a quest for the elusive cup; each loss was a heartbreaking lesson to learn for them, giving them the motivation to push harder. This hunger helped Ray achieve the best stats in his career, with 96 points, 31 goals, and 65 assists during the 1983-84 season. The best season of his career so far was doused in disappointment once more when the Canadiens prevailed over the Bruins in the Stanley Cup Semifinals.

Ray secured his name in the history books when he scored between 77 points and 95 points per game, with consistency, during the period between 1984–87, becoming the best defenseman in the league. He was appointed joint captain with Rick Middleton in the 1985-86 season, and the two of them continued to lead the team to the playoffs each season. And when Rick retired in 1988, Ray was made the sole captain. Ray led the team in victory against the Buffalo Sabres, Montreal Canadiens, and New Jersey Devils during the playoffs. This led to a face-off between Ray and the trio of Wayne Gretzky, Mark Messier, and Grant Fuhr; the odds were heavily stacked against Boston as the Edmonton Oilers won the Stanley Cup four games, defeating the Bruins in each one.

As captain, Ray won the James Norris Trophy in the 1986-87, 1987-88, and 1989-90 seasons as the best defenseman in the league. The team also had a good season during 1989-90 term—overriding Hartford, Montreal, and the Washington Capitals—bringing them face-to-face with the Oilers once again; it was a close repeat of their previous encounter, five games to one, with one of the games going into triple overtime in favor of the Oilers. Once again, Gretzky and company had shown the NHL universe who was the stronger team.

Ray continued to be invited to the All-Star games, and he won the James Norris Trophy twice more following the 1990-91 and 1993-94 seasons, becoming a household name throughout North America and Canada. He was the man who was decimated by the greatest players in hockey—twice—and walked out of the dressing room in the next seasons with his head held high and his eye on the Stanley Cup. Determination drove him to lead his team to consecutive playoffs, even if they fell short of winning the Cup, as was the case in the 1990-91 and 1991-92 seasons when the Pittsburgh Penguins hindered their path to the Conference Finals.

Even though Ray kept getting individual attention, his team was not as successful and didn't make the 1997 playoffs, a first since the 1960s. This was the culmination of a disappointing era. Professionally, and individually, Ray had won the Norris Trophy five times and had been invited to play in the All-Star teams 17 times, and received the King Clancy Memorial Trophy and the Lester Patrick Trophy. He was recognized as the third most successful defenseman, following Bobby Orr and Doug Harvey.

Age was not a defenseman's best friend, and as Ray neared his 39th birthday, he knew that time was running out for him to win the cup in his lifetime. At this point, Ray moved on from Boston as the longest-standing captain for the Boston Bruins, from 1988 to 2000, the longest in NHL history.

THE ULTIMATE SACRIFICE

Ray realized that he would possibly never achieve his dream if he stayed with the Bruins, even if leaving his adopted home wasn't what he had planned. He also hoped that a change of scenery would help him achieve this dream, and he requested to be traded—a request the management reluctantly agreed to. His teammates didn't see it as a betrayal, but rather an eye-opener. They had to lose the best player among them to understand the weaknesses and challenges that were holding them back from becoming winners. With a sad heart, Ray Bourque was traded to the Colorado Avalanche during the 1999-00 season.

Colorado fell short of winning the 1999-2000 season, losing to the Dallas Stars in seven games. The disappointment was bitter for Ray, but he instinctively knew that the Avalanches weren't so far off from achieving the ultimate dream. Ray kept hoping, keeping his team and fans holding onto hope, as well.

TENACITY WINS THE DAY

The 2000-01 season started with a bang, with Ray helping Colorado to the playoffs, accumulating 59 points. Facing the LA Kings, Vancouver, and St. Louis—Colorado powered through the playoffs, winning 12 games to 4, and meeting the New Jersey Devils. From Game 1, it was clear that the 2 teams were well-matched and equally determined to lift the cup. The Avalanches won Game 1—5-0, but lost Game 2.

Ray set another record by becoming the oldest player in the NHL when he scored the first goal in Game 3 at the age of 40, giving the Avalanches a 3-1 win. Games 4 and 5 went to the Devils, taking the win on the Avalanches' home ice. At this point, team energy and enthusiasm were waning, and the Avalanches were losing hope.

The coaches weren't sure what to tell the team, but Ray did. He gave the team the inspiration they needed by reminding them that there were possibly 2 games left—not only for the season but for him, as well—and that he was retiring after the final whistle blew. This was the turning point that the team needed.

Patrick Roy, the Avalanches' goaltender, won a career-highlight shutout when Colorado won the Devils 4-0 on their home turf in Game 6. This left both teams evenly contended for Game 7 in Denver. As the minutes ran down, Ray realized that the cup was within his grasp. With 11 seconds left on the clock and Colorado 3-1 in the lead, Ray Bourque was well on his

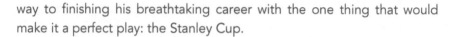

way to finishing his breathtaking career with the one thing that would make it a perfect play: the Stanley Cup.

THE BOSTON PARADE

Ray wanted to celebrate his achievement with the people who had adopted him, supported him, and still sang his praises when he entered the TD Garden arena. The mayor was all for a parade to celebrate with Ray, but the management of the Boston Bruins felt that Ray wanted to rub the cup in their faces. When Ray explained that it was about thanking the people who had given his career life, they reluctantly agreed. People came out in the thousands to watch their beloved hope-giver raise the visual achievement of all his hard work.

Ray Bourque was honored in many ways, given many accolades, set many records, and had many fan meets—but nothing could match the respect, acknowledgment, and honor shown to him by his captain, Joe Sakic.

After the obligatory picture for which Sakic held the trophy long enough to take photos, before the camera's flash stopped flashing, Joe held the metalwork out to Ray, allowing him to lift the cup 22 years after he debuted. The giant was forgiven for the tears streaming unashamedly down his face as he lifted the cup over his head.

TRIVIA FACT 1

At the start of his career, Ray wore number 7 to emulate his mentor, Phil Esposito. When Esposito retired in 1989, Ray changed his number to number 77, honoring his hero, as well as claiming his place in the NHL universe. The number 77 was retired by both the Boston Bruins, as well as the Colorado Avalanches when Ray retired—the first time a number was retired by more than one club.

TRIVIA FACT 2

Ray presented Boston with hope when every odd was against them, allowing them to keep reaching for their dreams. Ray never gave up on his dream, nor did he allow his fans to stop believing. He pushed his team to reach beyond their endurance level and to keep striving despite the bad press, the negative receptions, or the thought that they wouldn't make it. Just the fact that he was able to achieve the records he did inspired his team to keep breaking the glass ceiling.

He took this never-give-up attitude to the community that had accepted him as one of their own. Ray made it possible for struggling families to have a special Christmas by establishing the Bruins Christmas Toy Giveaway, providing gifts to many of their young fans. Ray was also the president of the board of a non-profit based in Boston that helped athletes raise funds for the causes close to their hearts. He was able to carry the candle of hope from the ice to the people who surrounded it.

CHAPTER 12

MATTIAS WEINHANDL —
A SAGA OF POWER OF VISION ON THE ICE

"Adversity is inevitable in life and sports. It's not about avoiding it but how you respond to it that truly defines you."

— Mattias Weinhandl

Born on June 1st, 1980, in Ljungby, Sweden, Mattias Weindhandl joined the junior hockey leagues and drew enough attention to his talent from the New York Islanders, who drafted Mattias in 1999. It would take him another 3 years before he made the transatlantic journey to don the colors of the Islanders. It took him some time to adjust to the smaller rinks and faster speeds of the American format of hockey compared to the wider rinks and slower pace of Swedish hockey.

Mattias impressed the general manager of the Islanders, Mike Milbury, with his ability to read the game and respond proactively. He not only created opportunities, but he also made sure that his teammates could push the play forward to escape a sticky situation. He was admired by his coaches and linemates, especially Alexei Yashin when Peter Laviolette, the coach of the NYI, gave him an audition.

Mattias enjoyed 4 seasons in the NHL, playing for the New York Islanders, a total of 182 games, 19 goals, 37 assists, and accumulating 56 points. He didn't have an immediate start on the ice when he joined the Islanders, playing more of a reserved position than an opener, but still being able to impress the NHL universe with his ability to maintain control of the puck despite his slight size in comparison to most of the other players. What also impressed Laviolette was Mattias's rare talent of being able to take possession of the puck in a scrimmage, anticipating where it would be and where to send it once he had it on his stick.

Laviolette moved on from the Islanders after the 2002-03 season, during Mattias's rookie year, and this meant that he got even less ice time than before. Between the 2002-03 and the 2004-05 seasons, Mattias shifted between the Islanders and the Bridgeport Sound Tigers in the AHL. He returned to Sweden for the 2004-05 season before going back to New York. The Minnesota Wild was able to win over Mattias in 2005-06, but he was once again relegated to the minor leagues during the 2006-07 season; he played for the Houston Aeros before returning to Sweden for a season and, then, being recruited into the Russian hockey league.

THE TRUE VALUE OF MATIAS WEINHANDL

Just after Mattias was drafted by NYI in 1999, he participated in the Four Nations Tournament representing his home country. During a match against the Czech Republic, Michal Travnicek hit Mattias in the left eye, putting his career at risk. Though Travnicek was suspended from international play for 36 months, Mattias nearly lost his career. As it was, he had lost 3 years of his NHL career because of the incident.

With the strong determination associated with the Swedes, Mattias underwent eye surgery at the end of the 1999-00 season. Using the off time to recover, Mattias returned to the Swedish Elite League, playing for MoDo for 48 games, finishing with 16 goals and 16 assists. To further demonstrate that he was fit for the ice, Mattias scored 18 goals and 16 assists in the 2001-02 season, making sure NYI didn't regret drafting him 3 seasons before.

Mike Milbury expressed admiration when he recounted the mindset of the Islanders' management when they heard about the injury, thinking that they might have to let Mattias go, but he surprised them with his tenacity. During the training camp, Mattias could match his teammates move for move, and even exceed their plays with maneuvers that shocked them. Alexei Yashin, the NYI center, was partnered with Mattias and could barely keep up with Mattias's offensive instincts and exceptional stick skills. The only thing that kept his play from being perfect was that he wasn't as fast as the American and Canadian players. The magic that made him good wasn't so much in the way he handled the puck or outplayed his opponents, but in the way he had recovered from an injury that could've ended his career, and returned to the game seamlessly. Yashin was surprised to learn that Mattias was in fact, 90% blind in his left eye. Milbury was very confident that Mattias could match Radek Martinek, one of the 4 top defensemen at NYI, and was unable to criticize Mattias's play or find weak spots in his technique.

CHANGING THE NARRATIVE

When Mattias learned that he wouldn't lose his eye, he accepted it as the best news because it meant he could still play. He was determined to be even better than he had been before the injury, overcoming any adversity he could with the skills and techniques that had made people take note of him. He took the incident as a means to grow, not only professionally but as a person; he recognized it as an opportunity to learn more about himself and how to become a better person and player. He managed to turn the experience into a positive.

How Mattias returned from his injury—not only physically, but professionally—had helped his coaches, like Peter Laviolette, have confidence in him. It showed that he was reliable on what he could offer in a physical sense, but how he was also able to read the game, anticipate his opponents, and know where to place the puck so that Mattias or one of his teammates could score. He could strategize a game plan on the ice, adjusting his play as the match evolved minute after minute. His contribution to the game has helped the Islanders achieve amazing results.

SWEDISH SUCCESS

Mattias played a year in Sweden after he finished his contract with the Minnesota Wild, joining Linkoping HC during the 2007-08 season, playing 54 games, and scoring 35 goals with 27 assists with a total of 62 points. That season saw Mattias recognized as the top goal scorer for the second time in the Swedish Elite Series. He signed a contract in 2008 with Dynamo Moscow and reached the semi-finals of the Gagarin Cup. He became a stalwart leader with his fellow linemates Petr Cajanek and Eric Landry—his presence domineering their opposing defensemen. Mattias scored 26 goals with 34 assists, accumulating 60 points in his second season which resulted in a 9-yr record. Mattias kept up the good form, being the first Swede to enter the newly established KHL. In 2010-11, Mattias moved to SKA St. Petersburg, with whom he scored 5 goals in the playoffs. He valued those games as it was during one of them that he scored against our infamous goaltender, Dominik Hasek.

His determination to be a better athlete than he was before his injury had kept his games consistent, scoring at least a goal or an assist per game. This meant that Mattias was chosen to represent Sweden during 5 World Championships (2001-02, 2004-05, 2007-08, 2008-09, and 2009-10), 3 Euro Hockey Tours (2007-08, 2009-10, and 2011-12), and the 2010 Winter Olympics.

Mattias's last World Championship with Sweden was an 8-1 victory over Denmark in which he had one goal and three assists, bringing the team to gold.

Mattias found himself back in his home country after he finished his contract with SKA, playing with Linkoping but not finishing the season with them

TRIVIA FACT

During the 2011-12 season, at the age of 33, Mattias made another courageous decision—to retire from hockey. This was after several seasons of hard impacts on the ice, as well as a direct hit that was the final knock and led him to his decision. He turned his opportunistic playing attitude to his investment and entrepreneurial company, helping other athletes make wise investments, not only financially but, also, in the community they practice their art in. The only involvement he had with hockey after his retirement was watching his sons play the game that brought him so much joy.

CHAPTER 13

ZDENO CHARA —
THE TOWERING GIANT

*"Being a leader isn't about being the loudest voice in the room.
It's about setting an example with your actions and your
dedication every single day."*

— Zdeno Chara

When you mention the name Zdeno Chara, the first thing that comes to mind is that tall dude who played for the Bruins. The 6 ft 9 in., 250 lb Slovakian national was born on March 15, 1977, in Trencin, Slovakia. He was told repeatedly by coaches that he was too tall to play hockey, and had changed teams thrice by the age of 16. His ability on the ice had attracted the attention of the New York Islanders. At the age of 19, he was the fourth pick in the third round of the NHL draft and was introduced to American hockey. During the 1996-97 season, the New York Islanders sent him to Prince George in the Western Hockey League before he was split between Kentucky of the American Hockey League, as well as the Islanders for the 1997-98 season.

"Big Z," as he was known in the NHL universe, had a reputation for being crafty, reliable, and vicious. He was a gigantic force that inspired fear and awe in his opponents, not only because of his size but, also, his speed and his ability to control the puck on the front and back of his stick, scoring with amazing power and accuracy.

THE SCARIEST MAN IN HOCKEY

The title of the "scariest man on the ice" was well-warranted as players—such as Henrik Lundqvist, Max Pacioretty, and many others—can attest to. Lundqvist had the misfortune of having a streaming puck strike him twice on the helmet and the second one—a shot by Chara—even broke his mask. Pacioretty was an unfortunate body check gone wrong and had broken a vertebra in the process with a severe concussion; Chara had served a five-minute penalty for the incident with no further actions to be taken against him after the video was reviewed. Chara had shown no fear when needing to defend his goal, whether it was by body checks, sticks, or even fists. The sheer size of Chara was enough to make an opposing forward think twice about challenging him on the ice, but his puck control and ability to shoot a puck at a hundred miles per hour or more in a quick slapshot had everyone clearing a path for Zdeno Chara.

Besides the fists and the power of 250 pounds rushing at you, what made Zdeno scary was the grace with which he skated, resembling a ballet dancer as he easily fulfilled the role of defenseman.

A role he perfected through his seasons with the Cougars and the Islanders, he used the early years in the NHL to find out what his long limbs were capable of, how to transform his height and weight to make his shots more powerful, how to cover the most ice with the most economical of movements, and how to preserve energy so that he could stay on the ice through all three periods without losing momentum.

Zdeno had been determined to play hockey because he enjoyed what the game offered him, and how the speed and intensity made him feel. He knew that he had to overcome the doubt that his youth coaches had filled him with, to work hard to become indispensable to his teams, and to show his coaches that he was more than just a tall, lanky young man who was all arms and legs. He wanted to prove to them that he could maintain a solid scoring ability as well as the fact that he had exceptional stickhandling talents. Zdeno found his place on the ice, leading more than just his teams to victory, but the community of the NHL.

FROM "CHOOSE ANOTHER CAREER" TO HERO

One has to wonder what the thoughts are of the man who coached a 16-year-old Zdeno and told him that he was too tall to play hockey, to then see him sharpen his skills—first for the Prince George Cougars, and then the New York Islanders—and win awards, setting records that are still standing in 2024. One also has to wonder what the thoughts of those coaches were when Zdeno was called to represent Slovakia in the World Junior Championship *after* he was called to play in the NHL.

Watching the big man dance around his opponents on the ice was like watching a ballet performance on stage. Zdeno learned to use his height to extract the puck from the opposing team's stick and send it up the ice to a teammate or the net itself. Because he demanded so much of himself, Zdeno pushed his teammates to keep up. Pushing himself physically, Zdeno could be found in the gym, not only during the season but during the summer, as well, where he worked out three times a day. He also constantly reviewed past games and strategies, considering how to implement them in future matches.

Chara had matured as a player and a person during his tenure at the Islanders, so the trade to the Ottawa Senators on June 23, 2001, allowed him the opportunity to put those lessons into practice. This determination garnered him an invitation to his first NHL All-Star Game in 2003. With the Senators, he scored 51 goals, 95 assists, and 146 points in the 296 games he played for them while he perfected his art as a defenseman. When the Senators released Zdeno as a free agent, the Boston Bruins signed him up immediately. He started on July 1st, 2006, and was appointed captain in October of that season, a position that he held until he went to the Washington Capitals 14 years later.

While holding the captaincy, Zdeno was awarded the Norris Trophy for being the top-ranking defenseman in the league in 2009, the first player from Slovakia to win this award. He was the second European-born player to lead his team to win the Stanley Cup in 2011, and made the NHL First-Team All-Stars three times. He also proceeded to win the Mark Messier NHL Leadership Award in 2010-11. In 2012, Chara set the record for the hardest slapshot at the All-Star Skills test at 108.8 mph, a record broken by Martin Frk in 2022 with 109.2 mph. His time at the Bruins saw Zdeno achieve several personal bests.

During his last season before his retirement in 2022, Zdeno Chara reached a milestone of 1,652 games, making him the leading defenseman with the number of games played. With each year, Chara pushed the team to improve their performances as much as he was determined to maintain his own form.

Zdeno had so much of an influence on the game that he agreed to a change to the usual Hardest Shot competition at the 2008-09 All-Stars. As he was the reigning champion for 4 years running, he challenged the NHL to donate $1,000 per player to a charity of the winner's choice. That year, besides winning the $24,000 raised for the event, he also won with a record 105.4 mph. He chose *Right To Play*, an organization that empowers children to rise above their circumstances by utilizing participation in sports, arts, and drama.

In the 2010-11 season, Chara achieved a rare feat for a defenseman by scoring his first hat trick against the Carolina Hurricanes, giving the Bruins a 7-0 victory and, ultimately, the Stanley Cup at the end of that season. In 2019, Zdeno became the oldest defenseman to score not only a game-winning goal during the playoffs but, also, an empty-net goal in the finals. He also became the oldest active player on the NHL roster, as well as the 21st player to play 1,500 games in the regular season.

Chara signed a one-day contract on September 20th, 2022, with the Boston Bruins to retire with the team where he found his niche.

Throughout his life, he did everything he could to prove his earlier coaches wrong. He took what they highlighted as a disadvantage and made it his strongest asset, using every inch of his size to prove to them that he was very capable of playing hockey. Zdeno's true strength didn't lie in his physical size, but in the way he didn't allow others to decide what he was capable of. He didn't allow others to place him in a box, stereotype him, or to limit him from achieving his dreams. He used the obstacles in his life as stepping stones to become one of the best defensemen the NHL has ever seen.

TRIVIA FACT 1

Zdeno uses a 67-inch stick that is 4 inches longer than regulation, especially allowed by the NHL to accommodate his height.

TRIVIA FACT 2

Zdeno has many passions outside of hockey. One of them is to give children a love for being active in sports, and not necessarily hockey, traveling as far as Mozambique to inspire future athletes to overcome their circumstances; he even climbed Mt. Kilimanjaro while he was in Africa. One way he contributed to nonprofits was by running in special events, including the Boston and London marathons. He is also one of the advocates of inclusionary hockey, giving everyone a fair and safe environment in which to play a game loved by millions, and unfolding gay players in the professional arena.

Zdeno Chara demonstrates daily that being a giant doesn't have to inspire fear because of his bodily size, but comradery because of the size of his heart.

CHAPTER 14

THE "MIRACLE ON ICE"

"Do you believe in miracles? Yes!"

— Al Michaels, the iconic call made by the American sportscaster during the final moments of the game between the USA and the Soviet Union at the 1980 Winter Olympics in Lake Placid.

Nothing is better than a Cinderella story, where the downtrodden person is pushed to the basement and the rest of the house party sparkles. This is the basis of the 1980 Olympics ice hockey event on February 22nd. The Soviet team would have been the stepsisters, winning all the medals, getting all the attention, and being drilled— *coached*—by the infamous Viktor Tikhonov.

They were the dominating force for anything to do with international hockey. The Russian team wore the crown as kings of the Olympics, as the gold medalists for four consecutive games under Tikhonov. The Soviet Union lineup resembled that of a Hollywood box-office movie, with names like Vladislav Tretiak in the net; Valeri Vasiliev and Sergei Starikov in defense; and Vladimir Krutov, Sergei Makarov, and Viktor Zhluktov as the formidable forwards. Not only talented players but combined with the exacting coaching styles of Viktor Tikhonov, as we discussed in Chapter 6, they were unstoppable.

The Americans had won a gold medal in the 1960 games with a silver in the 1972 Olympics and felt the pressure to finish first as they were playing on their home turf, in Lake Placid in New York. Head Coach Herb Brooks was no stranger to international hockey as he had participated in 3 Olympic teams, including the golden 1960 Games. He opted to fill the team with amateurs, mostly from Minnesota with an average age of 22.

WARM-UP UPSETS

The young American team meeting up with the Soviet team was a literal battle similar to the rookie facing off to Wayne Gretzky in his debut match. The dominance of the Soviets was evident at the exhibition game at Madison Square Garden as they thrashed the Americans 10-3, three days before the official match. The home team looked disorganized, uncoordinated, and uncertain; they seemed unprepared to face such a magnificent opponent, even after an intensive pre-Olympic exhibition series that included Europe since September 1979. Herb had ensured that they absorbed some of the techniques of the Europeans, especially the ever-moving weaving that was specific to the European teams.

VICTORY OF THE UNDERDOGS

Ranked number one, the Soviets fulfilled all expectations when they finished the first round with five wins, settling as favorites in the four-team medal round. The seventh-ranked U.S. team surprised everyone when they won four of the first-round matches and a tie.

Sweden was America's first opponent and was held at bay with a last-minute goal that tied their score at 2-2. The young Americans went on to displace Czechoslovakia, Norway, and Romania, with only West Germany left to play—the same team that had knocked America out of the 1976 Olympics, making them miss the bronze medal. Their nemesis took the lead in the first round with 2-0, but this was quickly tied in the second. The Americans took the lead in the third, winning the game 4-2.

Led by world-class goaltender Vladislav Tretiak, the Soviet team had decimated their opponents to meet the young American team. Both teams had entered their match with confidence, if not some arrogance on the side of the Soviets.

The sold-out arena audience wasn't disappointed. The Soviet team scored first, but Buzz Schneider evened the score halfway through the first period. Makarov pushed the Soviets' lead again before the period ended; however, Mark Johnson, once again, put the Americans on the scoreboard a second before the buzzer sounded.

In a moment of rare emotion, Viktor Tikhonov changed Tretiak for the inexperienced Vladimir Myshkin at the start of the second period. The Soviets pushed the play into the Americans' half for the period and managed to expand their lead with another goal early in the period— only thwarted from scoring more by goaltender Jim Craig. The third period started with Johnson scoring the equalizing goal as he took advantage of the Soviets' penalty.

The Americans took the lead with an eruption that had those in the arena on their feet when team captain Mike Eruzione (*eruption* in Italian) claimed a loose puck and sent it 25 ft down the ice with a spectacular wrist shot. Teamed with fantastic maneuvers from Craig, the Americans were able to keep the Soviets from scoring in the last 10 minutes of the game. The crowd called out the final seconds of the game and the American team and management staff filed onto the ice to celebrate. A very subdued Soviet team congratulated the Americans after the match. The irony of the game was that the Americans had used the passing techniques they had learned from the Soviets and combined them with the aggressive body-checking methods that put the Soviets off their game.

Riding the wave of victory, the Americans won their final match against Finland two days later.

A VICTORY ON ICE IS A VICTORY FOR ALL

Compared to the start of the Games, the immature squad had grown into a confident, well-balanced, and coordinated team that had members joining the NHL after the Olympics, carrying the title of being the best-conditioned American Olympic team of all time.

At the time of the 1980 Olympic Games, the USA had been going through political turmoil and confidence in the government was low. The Americans had planned to withdraw from the 1980 Summer Olympics in Moscow because of Russia invading Afghanistan. They were also faced with a recession, as well as the Iranian hostage crisis. Winning the gold medal was what the American citizens needed to have a glimmer of hope that things would become better.

NHL ROSTER ENTRIES

After the 1980 Olympics, 13 out of 20 of the players who participated in the *Miracle On Ice* match continued to play in the NHL. They went on to make great contributions to the league for many of the larger franchises. Below is a list of the men who made an impact in the last two games of the Olympics:

- Captain Mike Eruzione retired after the Olympics, leaving the ice on a high as he scored the winning goal.

- Defenseman Bill Baker scored the goal that tied the match with the Soviet team. He went on to play for the Montreal Canadiens, Colorado Rockies, St. Louis Blues, and the New York Rangers.

- Dave Christian was a prolific goal scorer in the 15 years of his NHL career, scoring 25 goals in a season eight times, as well as a career-high 41 goals in the 1985-86 season with the Washington Capitals. He also fulfilled the role of captain for the Winnipeg Jets.

- Steve Christoff scored the goal that brought the American team equal at 1-1 against Finland in the 1980 Olympic Final. He played five seasons in the NHL for the Minnesota North Stars with whom he had two 26-goal seasons, Calgary Flames, and the LA Kings.

- Neal Broten enjoyed 17 seasons in the NHL with the Minnesota North Stars (now the Dallas Stars) and went on to score the winning goal for the New Jersey Devils in the 1995 Stanley Cup Final against the Detroit Red Wings.

- Jim Craig had the honor of having the flag draped over him when America won the gold medal. He went on to play for the Calgary Flames, Boston Bruins, and the Minnesota North Stars in 30 games.

- Mark Johnson scored two goals against the Soviet team and played 11 seasons in the NHL with the Pittsburgh Penguins, Minnesota North Stars, St. Louis Blues, Hartford Whalers, and the New Jersey Devils. During the 1983-84 season, Mark scored 35 goals, the highest in his career.

- Rob McClanahan scored the winning goal against the Finns in the 1980 Olympic Finals and went on to play five seasons in the NHL for the Buffalo Sabres, Hartford Whalers, and the New York Rangers.

- Besides winning the Olympic gold medal, Ken Morrow also won the Stanley Cup Finals, the only player to do so in NHL history. He went on to win four consecutive Stanley Cup trophies with the New York Islanders in the 10 seasons he played with them.

- Mark Pavelich was instrumental during the match against the Soviets with 2 assists. He played 5 seasons with the New York Rangers where he was top-scorer in the 1982-83 season with 37 goals, Minnesota North Stars, and the San Jose Sharks.

- Mike Ramsey played for the Buffalo Sabres for 18 seasons before moving to the Pittsburgh Penguins and the Detroit Red Wings. He had also participated in the NHL All-Stars games, as well as the 1987 Rendez-Vous Series against the Soviet Union team.

- Dave Silk also assisted the USA's win against the Soviets with 2 assists. He played in the NHL for 7 seasons with the New York Rangers, Boston Bruins, Detroit Red Wings, and Winnipeg Jets with a career-high 15 goals in the 1981-82 season.

- The Soviet defenseman Vyacheslav Fetisov started appealing against the Soviet government's ban on players going to the NHL and was eventually successful after the fall of the Soviet Union—after they threatened to let him play in the Ukrainian minor leagues—and opened the door for many other Soviet players. Fetisov played for the Detroit Red Wings and won 2 Stanley Cups for them in 1997-98.

Besides uniting a country, all the men who played in the game that changed the opinions of the world about ice hockey will forever be remembered as the team that not only overthrew the Red Army, but they also showed the power of belief.

TRIVIA FACT

The Soviet team had won gold medals in five out of six Olympic Games—1956, 1964, 1968, 1972, and 1976. The only team to interrupt their winning streak was none other than the Americans in 1960.

CHAPTER 15

MARIAN HOSSA —
A MARTIAN'S JOURNEY TO WINNING
THE STANLEY CUP

"His work ethic and professionalism were second to none.
Marian Hossa was a leader both on and off the ice."

— Jonathan Toews

*T**ry and try and try again...***

This mantra embodies who Marian Hossa was: determined, focused, goal-orientated, and filled with perseverance. As a little boy visiting Canada during a pee-wee league tournament with his Slovak hockey club, Marian fell head over heels in love with the Chicago Blackhawks; he made it his lifelong goal to play for the team that held a roster full of his heroes, envisioning himself in the red, white and black holding the cup above his head—a dream his 11-year-old self used as motivation to succeed.

Marian Hossa was born in Stara Lubovna, Slovakia on the 12th of January, 1979 to a semi-professional hockey player father, Frantisek Hossa, who also coached the Slovakian National team, Zdeno Chara, Ziggy Palffy, Miroslav Satan, and Richard Zednik, and guided both his sons to play in the NHL. For Marian, when he was drafted by the Ottawa Senators in 1997, it was a stepping stone to his dreams coming true.

Raising his sons in a communist country, Frantisek didn't think that his sons would ever get out of Trencin; the communist Czechoslovakia didn't afford them much freedom of movement or speech, which had limited his career. He was relieved when communism fell in 1989 because it meant that the country was slowly releasing worthy players to the NHL and his sons could fulfill their careers outside of the Iron Curtain and have the freedom to move to America, where Marian joined the Senators and Marcel the Montreal Canadiens.

Frantisek was able to instill a sense of discipline and a good working attitude that Marian practiced to the day of his retirement, never missing a game to an opportunity to practice and following in his father's footsteps. Using this well-laid foundation, Marian mapped his path into the universe of the NHL.

CLIMBING THE STAIRCASE TO GREATNESS

After playing seven games with the Senators in the 1997-98 season, he was sent to play with the Portland Winterhawks in the Western Hockey League, who welcomed Marian into their team. It was a choice that had left Marian disappointed, though he didn't allow this to hold him back; he had dreams to achieve, after all. He opened himself up to absorb everything the team had to teach him, and Marian finished the season with 58 goals and 104 points in the 69 games he had played. This determination won him the Rookie of the Year while the team won the Memorial Cup, giving Marian continued confidence in his talent. He was brought back to the NHL and played with the Senators until the 2003-04 season when he was signed to the Atlanta Thrashers.

Hossa prided himself on his work ethic and made it a point to be technically sound in the way he played. It was with the Thrashers that he had 100 points during his second season. His biggest achievement while he was in Atlanta, though, was the establishment of his non-profit, *HOSS Heroes*, which helps underprivileged children, especially in his native country of Slovakia. He wanted to give everyone a chance to prosper and proposed that the owners of the Thrashers bring in more quality players to give the team a better chance at the playoffs, as well as bring more fans to the arena. The prospect was not financially possible, however, and he was traded to the Pittsburgh Penguins on February 26th, 2008.

KNOCKING ON CLOSED DOORS

At the Penguins, Marian briefly joined teammates Sidney Crosby and Evgeni Malkin during the 2007-08 season, working to get the team to win the Atlantic Division, as well as ending second in the Eastern Conference. This team also made it to the Stanley Cup finals against the Detroit Red Wings, but they lost game 6 with a score of 3–2, giving Detroit the fourth game win, and the 11th cup in their history. Not even the attempted goal from Crosby or the unsuccessful rebound from Marian could take the Penguins into victory.

This meant that Marian had to decide if he was going to try to win the cup with the Penguins again, or if he had to take his chances with another team. Despite being offered a lucrative deal to stay in Pittsburgh, as well as another offer by the Edmonton Oilers that was double that of the Penguins, Marian felt that he could learn more from players such as Datsyuk, Zetterberg, and captain Nick Lindstrom of the Detroit Red Wings and signed a one-year contract with them. This dispelled any assumptions that he chose the Red Wings because of money as he agreed to a pay cut when signing with them. For Marian, it was all about what he could learn to improve the quality of his play, especially how his defense improved when they played a post-practice game where they tried to take the puck off each other's sticks.

Once again, Marian reached the playoffs for the Stanley Cup in 7 games against his former team, the Pittsburgh Penguins. Their hopes were high as they won the first two matches, but then they lost the next two games, won Game 5, but lost Games 6 and 7, losing the Finals to the Penguins, the cup slipping through their fingers.

REACHING FOR THE STARS

Marian found a new home for himself when he signed a 12-year contract with the Chicago Blackhawks, one of the older members of the team dubbed the youngest in the NHL. This gave Marian the stability to perfect his game and focus on being a double-danger of a fast, sharp-shooting winger, as well as an effective defensive player. His previous season's 40 goals, 31 assists, and 71 points in the 74 regular season games would benefit the younger players as Marian filled a leadership role.

Adapting to the younger mindset of the Blackhawks' team was a challenge to Marian, but one he overcame with excitement as it showed him another side of hockey. The team was more playful when they were off the ice, though they were serious and formidable when the puck dropped.

Marian had been surprised by his new captain's confidence when he commented the evening before they were to play game 6 of the Stanley Cup Finals. Jonathan Toews had told him that when they won the cup, he was going to hand the cup to Marian first, honoring his time in the NHL as well as remembering that this would be Marian's third attempt at the cup in three years.

Chicago dominated the playoffs against the Philadelphia Flyers, winning 4 of the 6 games to win the final game 4-3 to take the Stanley Cup in front of the Philadelphia crowds. Everyone had waited with bated breath as the referees reviewed the last goal pushed over the goal line by Patrick Kane, with celebrations taking place as the last whistle blew. And true to his word, the Conn Smythe winner Jonathan Toews handed the cup over to Marian to the team's delight.

Marian went on to score his 1,000th point against his debut team, the Ottawa Senators, on October 30th, 2014, and his 500th goal against the

Philadelphia Flyers. He also holds the title of being the 8th NHL player to score 40 goals with 3 teams. He also became the first player to reach the Stanley Cup Finals with 3 teams in consecutive years, a feat recreated by Corey Perry 12 years later.

Marian's influence on the ice was unmistakable. His single-minded focus, determination, never-die faith, and dedication to every team he played for had helped those teams to reach not only the playoffs but the finals of the most prestigious trophy in any sport. By the time Marian was forced to retire, he had played a total of 1,309 games, scored 525 goals with 609 assists, and managed 1,134 points. Through all the years that he played hockey, including his childhood, Marian Hossa had dreamed of being a great hockey player, and he had achieved those dreams game by game.

Although a health condition forced Marian off the ice in 2017, he signed a one-day contract to retire as part of the Chicago Blackhawks in April 2022, the team that helped cement his reputation as a precision player and carve his name on the cup that every hockey player aimed for. Marian was inducted into the Hall of Fame in 2020 and honored in a ceremony on November 20th, 2022, when his number 81 was retired by the Chicago Blackhawks.

TRIVIA FACT

After getting close to the Stanley Cup twice before winning the trophy, Marian gave it a bit of his home country by filling the cup with pierogies, an Eastern European dumpling that can be filled with either cheese, fruit, or meat.

CHAPTER 16

MARIO LEMIEUX —
A CANCER SURVIVOR TURNING INTO
A COURAGEOUS SAVIOR

*"I never lost faith in myself. Every time I came back,
I came back stronger and more determined than ever."*

— Mario Lemieux

Lemieux was known as "the best," the most apt description for a man who drew attention since he put on his first pair of skates. From the many awards that follow his NHL stats to the perseverance, courage, and grit he showed to win the biggest fight of his life, Mario Lemieux exemplified the innocuous words: "the best."

Mario was born in Montreal, Quebec, on October 5, 1965, with two older brothers who enjoyed the game of hockey and taught him to skate at the age of two. This love was encouraged by their parents, who filled their front hallway with packed snow so that the boys could take every minute to practice. Mario played his first official game at the age of six and was showing true talent by the age of twelve.

With his eyes directed completely on hockey, Mario left school at 16 and proceeded to make his name in the Quebec Major Junior Hockey League (QMJHL). He scored 133 goals with 282 points when he was 18. He made sure that his name was remembered in the QMJHL by scoring 11 points in his final game. There was no alternative for the NHL than to have Mario in their first-round draft, and he was the first pick, going to the Pittsburgh Penguins.

Mario exploded into the NHL with a bang that would not be forgotten. October 11th, 1984, Mario debuted for the Penguins, scoring off the first time the puck hit his stick, on his first shift, getting number 66 onto the record sheets. He won Rookie of the Year for scoring 43 goals and 100 points. Word of his assertive play had spread through the NHL universe, drawing in the crowds like never before as the game attendance increased from 6,839 to 10,018.

Three years later, Mario teamed up with the *Great One*, scoring deftly off a Gretzky pass in the Canada Cup, claiming victory over a strong Soviet Union team, and winning the tournament. In the 1988-89 season, Mario just missed Wayne's 200 points per season, scoring 199 points with 85 goals and 114 assists—a career best.

Mario impacted every game he played in, setting the pace and ensuring that his teammates were on par. He surpassed Wayne Gretzky when it came to scoring goals and accumulating points, leading the Penguins to a Stanley Cup win in the 1990-91 season, with a repeat performance in the 1991-92 season. Mario ensured that he was on point when it came to goal accuracy, passing, puck control, and skating skills. He also used his height (6 ft 4 in.) as part of his tool kit, extending his reach across the ice, and covering more miles on the ice with each minute he skated. His hard work paid off when he was the leading scorer in the league 6 times, as well as winning the MVP 3 times, He also had the best stats for players with 150 games, scoring at least one point per game.

THE CRACKING OF THE ICE

Mario was riding the wave of a supersonic career, top of the scoring charts, media attention, and sold-out games with every season, especially after the Penguins won the Stanley Cup for 2 years running. At 27, he was one of the most recognizable faces on and off the ice. On January 12, 1993, the ice cracked beneath Mario's skates, leaving him and the NHL fandom in shock as he was diagnosed with Hodgkin's lymphoma.

UNDERSTANDING MARIO'S GREATEST NEMESIS

As a young man in his late twenties, Mario was within the group most at risk of Hodgkin's lymphoma, especially if there was a family history of this or similar cancers and if the person was HIV positive. As the illness finds its conduit through the body's lymphatic system, the white blood cells responsible for fighting germs in the body increase at an abnormal rate, depositing the excess into the lymph nodes situated in the neck, arm pit, and groin. If detected early, the chances of a full recovery are good, with the proper treatments of either chemotherapy, radiation, or a combination of both.

The excess deposits would result in swollen lymph nodes that would often not be painful, but tenderness or soreness may be experienced when drinking alcohol, and could be accompanied by constant tiredness. There may be a fever as the body tries to fight the possible illness, night sweats, and inexplicable weight loss. The fact Mario was able to maintain his stellar performance in the early stages of the illness speaks of his body being in pique condition, as well as the mental strength of an athlete at the top of his game, giving him a good stand on his journey to recovery.

Mario prioritized his health and took time away from the game he loved so much to undergo treatment after having a large lump removed from his neck. After two months of radiation therapy, Mario joined his teammates for their game against the Philadelphia Flyers where he scored a come-back goal with an assist. And he didn't slow down from there. Mario led the Penguins into a 17-game winning streak, reminding the NHL universe why he held the title of the best scorer in the league during the regular season. This was confirmed when he won the Hart Trophy for being the most valuable player in the league.

REPAIRING THE CRACKS

Besides the Hart Memorial Trophy, he also demonstrated his return by winning the Art Ross Trophy for the 160 points he earned during the 60 games he played. Just as Mario was reminding everyone about his skills, injury had him missing most of the 1993-94 season as a back operation for a herniated muscle kept him from the ice for the next season, as well. His return in the 1995-96 season had Mario scoring 161 points, and the season thereafter saw him scoring 122 points.

Mario decided that the 1996-97 season would be his last as his injuries wouldn't give him a break. By his last season, Mario had scored career 1,494 points, bringing him to sixth on the ranks of all-time scorers, allowing his early induction into the Hall of Fame in September 1997.

Mario spent 12 years giving the Penguins his most prestigious years, leadership, guidance, and skills—forging the reputation of a strategic center and sharpshooter, and making the Penguins the team to beat in the early 90s. So it was no surprise when he once again stepped up in 1999 and brought the crowds back home, just as he did as a player. Mario bought into the franchise with a few investors, taking up the role of owner and CEO. But being on the administrative side of hockey wasn't enough for Mario, and he pulled on his skates in 2000, realizing that he had more to give the team from the ice.

His return was heralded with 35 goals and 76 points in the 43 games he played. The 2001-02 season wasn't the best of his career as a hip injury only allowed him to play 24 games, seeing Mario score 6 goals. The one thing he could celebrate was that he was invited to captain the Canadian team, leading them to win their first Olympic gold medal in 50 years.

What stands out about Mario's return is that he dropped behind on the points log while he was out, having several players move ahead, but Mario used that as motivation to get his groove back instead of letting them overpower him. He used it as a means to propel him forward, even initiating a healthy rivalry between himself and Pat LaFontaine, gaining the lead with 12 points at the end of the regular season. Even being an owner of the Penguins didn't slow him down, scoring 3 points in his return match, setting the rhythm for the next 2 seasons when he, once again, was the leader in points per game.

Not only is Marion known as the "Magnificent One," but also as the "Comeback King" as he seemed to return with more energy, more determination, and more drive to win. It's as though he found himself invincible after overcoming cancer and was determined to make his presence known and unforgettable—as though he was making sure that his name was synonymous with being victorious. Mario showed his mettle on the ice when he skated rings around his opponents, scored magnificent goals, and broke records as though they were eggs for an omelet. He displayed his respect for Gretzky, a man who would be his nemesis in the record-making market, and he drew in the crowds that were a large part of any franchise's income. He saved the franchise, not only in popularity as a player or financially as an owner, but as a survivor inspiring many others in their fight against cancer.

Together with John Cullen who was diagnosed with non-Hodgkin's lymphoma, Maurice "the Rocket" Richard who was diagnosed with abdominal cancer, and Paul Stewart (colon cancer), Mario and these three were the faces behind the NHL's "Hockey Fights Cancer" initiative that runs through October and November each year, raising funds to donate to cancer research and treatment, including the entire NHL universe, throughout the world.

TRIVIA FACT 1

His experience with cancer made him aware of the plight that many patients and their families endure while they undergo treatments, and Mario established the Mario Lemieux Foundation in 1993. The foundation raises funds to support families to get the best treatment they can find. *Austin's Playroom* was later added to the foundation's services after Mario's son, Austin, had to be in the Neonatal Intensive Care Unit for three months.

The foundation has raised millions of dollars for cancer research and patient care. In the 31 years that the Foundation has been established, there were approximately 43 Austin's Playrooms set up across the country, assisting 1.5 million families. The foundation also supports the Mario Lemieux Center for Blood Cancers, Immunotherapy Center, Lymphoma Center, and the Institute for Pediatric Cancer Research in the Pittsburgh area.

TRIVIA FACT 2

Mario Lemieux won the Stanley Cup five times, twice as a player in 1990-91 and 1991-92, and three times as an owner in 2009, 2016, and 2017, the only person to win it as a player and an owner.

CHAPTER 17

BOBBY BAUN —
A BOOMER ONCE TRANSCENDING
FLESH AND BONES

"In the face of pain, there are two choices: succumb or persevere.
I chose to lace up my skates and keep fighting, for my teammates,
for my fans, and for the love of the game."

— Bobby Baun

Robert "Boomer" Baun was born on September 9th, 1936, in Saskatchewan, and displayed exceptional defensive skills at a very young age. Physically, he wasn't a very large man, but he could place a shot stronger than a man twice his size, giving him the nickname "Boomer." He had no issue checking a forward to ensure that the Toronto Maple Leafs won the game.

Bobby had grown up in the Maple Leafs Junior B Weston club before moving on to the major junior team, Toronto Marlboros. This prepared him to play in the professional league, although he played only 20 games for Toronto during the 1956-57. He joined the Rochesters in the American League and played another 46. The 1957-58 season saw Bobby playing for the Leafs full-time.

Bobby's inelegant skating had many opponents underestimating his strong stick work, goal-stopping, and the force of his hits. Though many forwards could outskate Bobby, he was able to body-check the player in open ice or take them away from the Leafs' goal crease. He didn't hesitate to engage with anyone daring to approach the net. He was quick to defend his teammates without considering the consequences. An example of this was the match against the Chicago Blackhawks on December 7th, 1963, when the Leafs were three goals ahead, the opposing Reggie Fleming speared Bobby's teammate, Eddie Shack. Bobby dropped his gloves and engaged with Fleming late in the third period.

Both Fleming and Bobby were sent from the ice for the fight. Bobby would eventually earn 25 minutes of the Leafs' 69 penalty minutes that the referee had handed out during that match, with the Blackhawks earning the other 86 minutes of the overall 155 penalty minutes of the game. He was additionally fined $2,800 for game misconduct. Conn Smythe, the owner of the Leafs, replaced the fine with a check to Bobby for Christmas. The letter accompanying the check said that Smythe expected men to be counted and to stand up, commending Bobby for his grit on the ice.

STICKS AND BONES

With a recorded 964 games with 37 goals and 187 assists, Bobby had accumulated 224 points as well as 1489 penalty minutes, affirming his reputation of being a hard hitter. He had 17 regular seasons in the NHL, from 1956 to 1973, giving all of his skills and even his body, to winning the game. In the 96 playoff games he had played in, Bobby scored 3 goals, and 12 assists, and spent 171 minutes in the penalty box.

He spent 14 seasons with the Toronto Maple Leafs (1953- 1967) and won four Stanley Cups with the team—1961-62, 1962-63, 1963-64, and 1966-67—with Bobby playing significant roles in all of them, but nothing could overshadow the events of the 1963-64 finals, where Bobby Baun made his position clear in the Toronto Maple Leafs.

The Leafs were behind in the series, 2 games to 3 against the Detroit Red Wings. Game 6 saw Bobby spend time in the penalty box during 2 of the Red Wings' 3 goals. With the two teams drawn at 3-3, Bobby stepped in front of a Gordie Howe shot with just over 15 minutes on the clock in the third period. When he went to face-off with Gordie, he collapsed and had to be stretchered off the ice.

After confirming that it didn't need emergency treatment, the medical team iced his ankle, strapping it tightly, and Bobby returned to the ice to play in overtime. This was enough time for Bobby to score the winning goal, taking the play into Game 7. Bobby played Game 7 with intermittent pain injections into his injured ankle and joyously lifted the cup with his team when they won 4-0.

Bobby was the embodiment of dynamite coming in small packages, and had the opposing teams skating wide berths around him, mostly to avoid his stick, fist, or whatever he could use to clear his goal crease. He wasn't afraid of the isolation of the penalty box, and would gladly sit there if it meant his team won. What made him even scarier was that he wasn't just a brute. Bobby could devise ways in which to score goals, as well as open opportunities for his teammates to score.

The ankle injury couldn't slow Bobby down, even when—two days after the Stanley Cup win—they took x-rays and discovered that he had broken his ankle. Just weeks after the ankle was plastered, he soaked the cast in a bathtub until it came off, allowing him not to diminish his presence on the ice. After winning the 1966-67 Stanley Cup, his fourth with the Leafs, Bobby was traded with five of his teammates in May 1968. His reputation followed him to the next two teams, the Oakland Seals and the Detroit Red Wings.

While playing for the Seals, Bobby injured his neck, but continued to play as though he was 100% fit, still giving hard body shots and aggressive blocks. He then returned to the Leafs for the 1970-71 season where he played the last years of his career. His 1972-73 season wasn't his best, as he collided with Mickey Redmont of the Detroit Red Wings, which injured his neck in the fifth game of the season. He admitted that the initial injury had happened 5 years previously, while he was playing for the Oakland Seals, and that he had been playing with a broken neck since then. He had been given the option of having surgery, but it came with a great risk of paralysis or retiring to avoid another injury that could also leave him in a wheelchair.

When Bobby died on August 15th, 2023, the Toronto Maple Leafs president Brendan Shanahan described Bobby as the player who embodied the character and values of hockey. His resilience was iconic to his games, where not even injury could keep him off the ice. He especially remembered Bobby defining his role on the ice as someone who needed to stop goals and if he scored one, then it was a bonus.

Bobby believed that he needed to respect his fans and endeavored to sign as many autographs as he could. He reasoned that if a fan could take the time to wait for a player, he could take the time to sign their jersey. This showed the ultimate respect that Bobby had for his craft and the fans that followed his career.

TRIVIA FACT

In 1962, the Toronto Maple Leafs played against the New York Rangers. This coincided with Queen Elizabeth II's tenth year on the throne, and during a vibrant rendition of "God Save The Queen" before the game, someone tossed a device toward the Leafs' bench, setting it off close to where Bobby and linesman Matt Pavelich were located. Though Pavelich's jersey suffered some burns, both men were blinded for a few seconds but not injured.

People assumed that it was a firecracker, but the police ruled that it was a bomb that had been flung at the bench. The arena had been too dark for anyone to see who had tossed it, though. The game went on, and Bobby played as if it was a normal game, even being sent to the penalty box in the second period for two minutes. The incident had the Leafs improving the security measures at their home arena, starting with having more lights on during the opening ceremonies.

CHAPTER 18

DOUG JARVIS —
THE IRON MAN OF ICE HOCKEY

"I may not have been the flashiest player on the ice,
but I took pride in doing the little things right. Attention to detail
and hard work were the keys to my success."

— Doug Jarvis

A product of Brantford, Ontario, Douglas Jarvis was born on March 24th, 1955. He was a neighbor of the great Wayne Gretzky and a fellow pupil of Walter Gretzky's Junior B team. Until the age of eight, Doug had never skated in a closed arena. Doug could be found on the baseball field or the lacrosse pitch when the hockey season ended. Though hockey held a special place in his heart from an early age, he took advantage of getting to know the ethics of other sports and widening his friendship base.

He was drafted to the Peterborough Petes because of his offensive talent in 1972, enjoying three seasons with them, and had the privilege of being the captain for Canada at the 1974 World Junior Championship. The coach of Peterborough, Roger Neilson, expected his players to know the ice and be capable of playing every inch of it. By the end of his third season, Doug had played 202 games—scoring 96 goals, 190 assists, and 286 game points.

With the 1975 NHL draft, Doug was the 24th overall pick, chosen by the Toronto Maple Leafs, though the Houston Aeros of the WHA also showed an interest. He was on the Leafs roster for a month when he was traded to the Montreal Canadiens, something that Doug wasn't too disappointed about as they had been his favorite boyhood team. Doug had the skills that the Canadiens needed to fulfill their star lineup, especially because he could fill a defensive role with the ability to face off.

The Hall of Fame lineup of the Canadiens won four Stanley Cups in 1976, 1977, 1978, and 1979; Doug's spot was undisputedly cemented on the team. A teammate described Doug as a strong motivator, inspiring them to give their best every time they went on the ice, and constantly pushing them to maintain their physical peak. After 560 games with the Canadiens, Doug had scored 91 goals and 154 assists with 245 points, Doug Jarvis had not missed a single game for the Montreal Canadiens.

He was traded to the Washington Capitals during the 1982-83 season; a year later, Doug won the trophy coveted by all defensemen: the Franke J. Selke Trophy. Doug wasn't an imposing person in size at 5 ft 9 in., but he was described by opponents and teammates as being a solid presence who could manipulate the space on the ice so that the other team stayed out of the Canadiens' goal zone. During this time, he had the honor of playing against his former teammate, Wayne Gretzky—as well as every player's hero, Gordie Howe—when he returned to the NHL for his last season in 1979-80, a personal highlight of his career.

During the 1985-86 season, Doug was traded to the Hartford Whalers, once again participating in all of the 25 games up to his trade, and then the 57 games left in the regular season with the Whalers.

During the Christmas Eve match of 1986, Doug broke even with Garry Unger, who had finished his season from 1968 to 1979 with 914 games. Doug passed this record at the Boxing Day match against his first NHL team, the Montreal Canadiens, making his total 915 games.

INVINCIBLE IRON MAN

Doug never intended to be a record breaker. His main goal was to be on the ice and do what he enjoyed the most: play hockey. Doug wasn't as flashy as his compatriots during that era of hockey, where scoring goals and brawling were as much a part of the game as donning the team jersey. Understated, Doug had only scored 20 goals during his last season with the Canadiens, the highest in his long career—and he rarely got involved in fights on the ice, having only accumulated 34 minutes in one season in the penalty box, at most.

Doug played from 1975 to 1988, a total of 964 games without missing a single one despite injuries and illnesses. Hockey is a physical game, and if a player wasn't injured on the ice at some point in his career, he wasn't doing it right; however, the one thing that *can't* be said about Doug is that he couldn't play hockey properly. He had missed four Stanley Cup finals because of injuries. As playoff matches fell under a different category to the regular games, those off-ice matches weren't part of Doug's record. There were two injuries that *nearly* kept Doug off the ice— an ankle injury in the 1980s and a more serious head injury that had him spending a night in the hospital while he still played for the Capitals. Fortunately, Doug was able to overcome both injuries to maintain a continuous streak of game participation.

It was only during his last season that his number of appearances decreased because Jack Evans, the Whalers' head coach, realized that Doug had been playing very hard for all his career and they needed to release him to extend his playing years. This also allowed for the more youthful Brent Peterson to get more game time.

This led to Doug moving from the NHL to the AHL, where he played for the Binghamton Whalers before he officially retired.

ALL RECORDS MUST BE BROKEN

Doug's 964 game streak was strong until the 2021-22 season, where it was passed by first, Ketih Yandle of the Philadelphia Flyers, who would be playing against the New York Islanders, and who finished with 989.

Both Doug's and Keith's streaks were overtaken by Phil Kessel of the Vegas Golden Knights with an astounding 1,064 game-streak. If the Knights signed Phil on for another season, his number would increase.

What these three strongmen had in common was that they didn't play to beat the current streak. They weren't intent on beating someone's record. That was not a part of their focus. Though their milestones were acknowledged, it was the honor to play as long as they could with minimal injury that made them appreciate their accomplishments. For Doug, it was about being on the ice. It was about fulfilling his role for his teammates, giving a quality game for his fans, and showing his coaches that he respected their input into his techniques. Doug's determination, integrity, skills, and sportsmanship was well-lauded by everyone he played *with* and *against*. And for Doug, it was about knocking his friend and former teammate, Wayne Gretzky, from his lofty pedestal.

TRIVIA FACT

Doug has put his tenacity and determined streak to good use after he retired. Besides coaching for more than 31 years, he also participates in long-distance races and several marathons. He has also passed on these characteristics, techniques, lessons, and values he had learned from the many coaches who had influenced his life.

CHAPTER 19

OVECHKIN VS. CROSBY — THE RIVALRY OF THE GENERATION

"Playing against Ovi is always a challenge. He's got a shot like nobody else, and you have to be ready for it every time he's out there."
— Sidney Crosby

"Sid's one of the best players in the world. Every time we face each other, it's a battle, but it's also a lot of fun."
— Alex Ovechkin

Occasionally, two players will match each other in skill, capability, and goal-scoring prowess—two players who can outmaneuver any other player except each other, and are both recognized as the next great player. Both players captain their respective teams. Both players have thrashed their way through the junior leagues with nothing but sheer determination, hard work, and natural talent. Can we compare them to Wayne Gretzky and Mark Messier? Let's meet the "Titans of The New Generation."

ALEX "OVI" OVECHKIN

Born in Moscow, Russia, on September 17th, 1985, to a professional soccer player father and gold medalist basketball player mother, Alexander Mikhaylovich Ovechkin grew up in a modest part of the city. He used hockey to escape the crumbling area around them and the strict public school he attended. Encouraged by his older brother, Sergei—a professional wrestler who died in a car accident—Alex focused on hockey to help him find a better life for himself, avoiding the drug traps his friends were falling into.

With this focus, he became the youngest member of the Russian national team after getting his start with Moscow Dynamo at the age of 16. Alex proceeded to score 14 goals in 8 games at the under-18 World Championship held in Slovakia in 2002. He garnered the attention of the NHL scouts, aligning with Alex's main goal as he considered the NHL the best in the world. The Florida Panthers had been aware of his talent for some time and did all they could to draft him as their first pick in 2003, but his birthday was 2 days after the cut-off date, preventing Alex from joining the vibrant team. When he was called the next year as the first pick in the NHL 2004 draft by the Washington Capitals, it was a dream come true.

Alex had to patiently wait for this dream to materialize, as the NHL had a lockout in the 2004-05 season, resulting in Alex missing his official debut season. He entered the scene with his powerful slapshots in his first match in October 2005, to score 2 goals in 4 minutes and give a body check to an opponent, which broke the partitioning. Alex was awarded the Calder Memorial Trophy for the Rookie of the Year when he scored 52 goals and 54 assists.

SIDNEY "SID THE KID" CROSBY

Born on August 7th, 1987, Sidney Patrick Crosby was born in Cole Harbor, Nova Scotia. His father was drafted by the Montreal Canadiens, a team that held a special place for Sidney in his early years, and he idolized Steve

Yzerman. He learned to skate by age three and was a recognized talent by the time he was seven, conducting interviews with the local media. His father had set up a net in their basement next to his mother's dryer, which became a victim of Sidney's hours of shots into the net, the dented appliance holding a place of honor in the Nova Scotia Sports Hall of Fame.

His hardworking determination carried him through his career in the minor leagues, on Dartmouth Subways team in the Nova Scotia Major Midget Hockey League in 2001-02. Sidney is still the record holder with the club for the number of goals, assists, and points—scoring 193 points in the 74 games he played with them. In the next season, Sidney played with the Shattuck-St. Mary's Preparatory School in Minnesota, a school that had seen several NHL players, including Jonathan Toews and Nathan MacKinnon, skate on their ice. The Rimouski Oceanic of the Quebec Major Junior Hockey League (QMJHL) recruited Sidney at the end of that season. In the two seasons he played for the Rimouskis, Sidney had an outstanding 303 points, leading the league, as well as earning the Player of the Year title.

With the 2005 draft pick, Sidney was the first pick, easing into the NHL with confidence as he scored 39 goals and 102 points in his debut season with the Pittsburgh Penguins. Sidney made sure that his name was in the annals of the NHL at a very early stage in his career by being the youngest player to score 100 career points (at age 18), as well as the milestone of 200 points by the time he was 19, breaching Wayne Gretzky's record by 140 days. He missed out on earning the Calder Trophy for Rookie of the Year by the "big Ovi." He also had the honor of becoming the youngest captain in the NHL when taking over the role in 2007.

THE RIVALRY OF THE GENERATION

The NHL had a lockout during 2004-2005, leading to Ovi playing in his first match in the 2005-2006 season, ultimately debuting at the same time as Sidney. Both players instantly caught the attention of their respective teams' fans.

Already, with many years of experience in the NHL and with many more years of playing—injuries aside—to come, both Ovi and Sidney have proven themselves in their roles of captains. Each of them has also surpassed records set up by giants—such as Wayne Gretzky, Mark Messier, Mario Lemieux, and others—and both have led their teams to Stanley Cup wins. Ovi was the first Russian to captain a team to hold the Cup, while Sidney was the youngest captain in NHL history to do so at the age of 21.

Is there something that sets them apart? Both Sidney and Alex are prolific point scorers, but Alex takes the lead in goals while Sidney's points are mostly made of assists. Both of them use the ice with effective accuracy, opening up alleys for their teammates to push the play forward, ready to either score goals or create opportunities to score. They have each won much-coveted trophies—including the Art Ross Trophy, the Conn Smythe, Hart Memorial, Ted Lindsay, and the Maurice 'Rocket' Richard Trophy—which is inevitable for two forwards with similar skill and ability, both driven to be the best in the sport and with similar work ethic.

They are both team-driven, wanting the best for their teams, whether it is a cup-winning season or to have their team in the playoffs. They are both team-orientated, helping their teammates achieve the best seasons of their careers in the way of assists or being injury-free. They both play the game with focus, not concentrating on the records they are breaking or the giants they are leveling as they move from game-to-game, season-to-season. Though fiercely competitive on the ice, both men are inherently sportsmen, meaning they have only mentioned each other with the utmost respect in terms of their sport and person.

Besides leading their teams on the ice, they are also community-minded. Alex is the ambassador for the American Special Hockey Association (ASHA), helping them to increase the number of players to 8,300 and bringing in enough donations so that ASHA could cover the cost of the ice for 136 teams across the country.

Every year, Sidney returns to his hometown of Cole Harbor, where he hosts young hockey players at his school for a week, teaching them on- and off-ice skills, as well as having peers in hockey giving presentations to the kids. His charity, the Sidney Crosby Foundation, also supports other charities in the Nova Scotia area, reaching children and their families in the maritime area.

CHAPTER 20

THE PANTHERS —
THE RAT TRICK ON THE ROSTER
OF THE RINK

"We were scoring a lot of goals and they were a big part of the playoffs. That's something people remember."

— Scott Mellanby, former Florida Panthers player who famously scored two goals in the Panthers' first home game of the 1995-1996 season, leading to the rat-throwing tradition.

Rats. Sticks. Fans. And a new tradition was started.

Named after the endangered southern Florida felines (also known as cougars or mountain lions), the *Florida Panthers* were established in 1993. They entered the Eastern Conference and finished their first two seasons by qualifying for the Stanley Cup playoffs. The 1995-96 season saw the young team knock the top two teams out of the conference to play in the Stanley Cup finals against the Colorado Avalanches. The Panthers lost against the stronger Avalanches; though the Panthers reached the playoffs again in the next season, they were knocked out in the first round.

THE NEW RAT PACK

October 8, 1995, would be branded into the minds of players and fans alike in the Miami Arena, giving the Florida Panthers a clear path to the Stanley Cup finals.

Before stepping onto the ice for their game with the Calgary Flames, the Panthers were sitting in their locker room when a tiny fan joined them: a four-legged creature that would have many people jumping on their chairs—a rat. Instead of cowering, though, Captain Scott Mellanby showed his supreme leadership skills by grabbing a stick and, with a well-placed shot, hit the rat against a wall that tragically ended its life. This incident sparked a change on the ice and the Panthers won the match with a resounding 4-3 victory over the Calgary Flames—two of those goals coming off the same stick that Scott used to dispatch the rat.

After the match, the goaltender, John Vanbiesbrouck, relayed the story to the press and referred to Scott as making a "rat trick." The episode created a new tradition because the next evening, a fan tossed a toy rat onto the ice at a Panthers goal during the New Jersey Devils game; it became the new celebration. This became the biggest intimidation tactic for fans to opposing goaltenders, sending them cowering into their nets. It also established a partnership between the Panthers and Orkin, an extermination company that would send their teams onto the ice to "exterminate" the tossed toys.

The trend was so popular that the rats were sold at the arena before the games; the NHL stepped in and asked the Panthers to stop selling the toys. Eventually, the team asked the fans to throw the toys only if the team had won, and *not* during the match. As a result, the NHL made a new rule that the teams could face minimal penalties if toys were tossed onto the ice before the final whistle.

As with most teams, the Panthers suffered a few seasons of disappointment, and, as the goals and points dried up, so did the tradition. Fewer and fewer rats were flung to the ice until the 2015-16 season.

To gain support from the fans, the Panthers management distributed 10,000 toy rats to the fans entering the arena as a promotional gimmick. The excitement of the fans was too much for them to abide by the rules, and the rats went flying onto the ice during the match, leading to 2 team penalties of 2 minutes each, to the chagrin of superstar Jaromir Jagr. Fortunately, New Jersey wasn't able to capitalize on the advantage, and the Panthers won the game 3-2.

Though the Panthers appealed the penalties, the NHL rule was stronger than the team's conviction, and they lost the appeal. Jaromir was convinced that, though they had won this particular match, nothing was stopping one of their opponents from hiring someone to buy a toy and toss it on the ice, with that team possibly taking advantage of the penalty against the Panthers.

TO TOSS OR NOT TO TOSS

This is, of course, not the first time that fans tossed their favorite toys on the ice to show their appreciation for their team's performance.

The Detroit Red Wings fans took the tradition a little too seriously when they tossed actual octopi on the ice. This was started in 1952 by the Cusimano brothers, who owned a fish market. Pete Cusimano threw an octopus on the ice to celebrate the Red Wings' goal in the third game of the Stanley Cup playoffs against the Montreal Canadiens. The mollusk was to represent the eight playoff wins that a team needed to win the Stanley Cup at that time. It became a norm for Cusimano to throw an octopus onto the ice after Detroit scored the first goal.

When the Red Wings played against the New Jersey Devils in April 2017, 35 octopi were thrown onto the ice during the last game to be played in the Joe Louis Arena before they moved to their new home. The tradition has not changed much during the ensuing years, except that real octopi were swapped with stuffed ones.

TRIVIA FACT

Though the NHL discourages fans from tossing anything on the ice during the matches, some minor league clubs have taken the tradition and given it a philanthropic twist. One such club is the Hershey Bears in the AML.

On January 7th, every year, they have a tradition termed *the teddy bear toss* started in 2001, where fans toss thousands of teddy bears on the ice after the Hershey Bears' first goal. These toys are then donated to 35 local charities supported by the team's Hershey Bears Cares program. In 2023, 67,309 bears were collected; in 2024, this total amounted to 74,599. Since 2001, 464,107 bears have been collected in this way.

THE 334 CLUB
Devils 7, Calgary 5
January 22, 1987
MEADOWLANDS ARENA

CHAPTER 21

NJD 334 CLUB —
THE TALE OF FEW

*"The storm may have kept some away, but for those of us
who braved the elements, being part of the NJD 334 Club is a badge
of honor. We were there when it mattered most."*

— A devoted Devils fan who attended the game.

Throughout the book, we've discussed the importance of commitment and dedication: whether it's a player to his craft, like Connor Bedard; dedication to his fans, like Bobby Baun; or the love and support of the everlasting fans, like those of the Detroit Red Wings throwing octopi on the ice. Being a die-hard fan is a commitment that few can achieve. Dressing up, having the logo or mascot tattooed on your body, or traveling to all the away games are fine examples of being a dedicated fan. But would you risk a blistering Nor'easter to support your team?

January 22, 1987, was an important game against the Calgary Flames, and the Devils' management estimated a large crowd, as more than 11,000 tickets were sold. Instead, the temperatures dropped and a blizzard blew in, laying down 3 in. of snow an hour; the snow was heavy enough to shut down the entire city. There were concerns that the match might have to be canceled, as the roads had become hard to use. Any attendance from the players, staff, and fans was doubtful.

The players had trickled to the arena; one of them even walked one-and-a-half miles to the arena when he was stuck behind an accident, but another had fortunately arrived earlier. The chartered bus of the Flames had also left their hotel earlier than scheduled and arrived at the arena before the snow became a menace. They had to wait for a face-off, as none of the match officials had arrived yet. Eventually, one linesman was able to make it through and was closely followed by several of the other Devils' players—one of them having reversed to the rink when he had to avoid a snow drift.

The fans, one driving from Long Island on different routes to get there, the 22-mile route taking nearly five hours, walked into a surreal situation. The sight of them surprised the players, who had not expected anyone to attend. Nick Fotiu, the Flames forward, tossed pucks to them in appreciation of their dedication to the team. Ken Daneyko, the Devils' defenseman, later recalled that it felt like a practice session to him, especially when every sound from the ice reverberated around the arena in response to the emptiness.

With a referee and more Devils players in attendance, the game was able to begin 105 minutes later than the scheduled start time. Larry Brooks, the public relations director and vice president of communication for the Devils, chatted with each of the fans and took down their names and addresses.

The game opened with a goal from the Devils' Perry Anderson; he wasn't scheduled on the original roster but, because they needed to fill positions, he was called up. The third period saw the Flames leading by 4-3, but the Devils remedied that within six minutes. Doug Sulliman was also on the scoreboard with a hat trick, the only one of his career, to help the Devils win the match 7-5 against one of the stronger teams in the NHL. Doug had to throw his own baseball cap on the ice after his hat trick because it had been too cold for the fans to toss theirs.

One of the newspaper headlines stated that not even a blizzard or the Flames could keep the Devils at bay. Few newspaper headlines had reported that the Devils had overthrown one of the more powerful teams in the NHL at that time. Few of them detailed Sulliman's hat trick, and that it was the only one of his career. Few of those headlines included the risk the players took to be present for their fans. And even fewer applauded the dedication displayed by not only the players or fans, but also the management staff, game officials, off-ice staff, and media.

The thing that was remembered about that match wasn't the 7-5 score, nor the fact that the Devils had been beaten by the Flames for a while in the game, trailing behind, before racing ahead of them. It was the sacrifice, dedication, and commitment of the fans who attended that stole the show. It was those fans who demonstrated what it meant to be "die-hard." It was those fans who gave the teams, both the Devils and the Flames, the motivation to give their best efforts to a game that might never have happened.

The number of fans who had made it to the game totaled just 334. It might be a low number for a normal game, but it was a huge triumph over dangerous conditions in order to rally for their teams!

True to Larry Brooks' word, the Devils inducted those 334 fans into an exclusive club: the *334 Club*. Each of them received a gift box containing a letter, a pin, a T-shirt, and tickets to the next game between the Devils and the Flames, or closest to the January 22nd anniversary of this game. In addition, they attended a dinner and drinks on the anniversary every year. They have also received an invitation to a game and a private reception on the 25th anniversary.

TRIVIA FACT

The game between the New Jersey Devils and the Calgary Flames still holds the record for the lowest attendance ever in NHL history with 334 fans in attendance.

YOUR OPINION MATTERS TO US!

Hey there, Friend and Fellow Hockey Enthusiast!

You've just flipped through the final pages of our hockey adventure together. We're beyond thrilled you chose to join us on this journey, diving into the heart and soul of the game we all adore. You know, putting this book together was like preparing for a big game: it took loads of passion, a bit of nerve, and a whole lot of love for hockey.

Now, we're reaching out with a small but super important request. If you enjoyed your time with us, could you share your thoughts in a review? Whether it's a shoutout, a bit of love, or even some ways you think we could up our game, your feedback is golden. It helps us reach more fans like you and, honestly, it keeps our spirits high and the motivation burning to bring even more hockey tales to life.

So, grab a moment, drop us a few lines, and let's make this hockey community even more vibrant together.

Thank you for every cheer, every gasp, and every quiet moment spent with our book. You're not just a reader; you're part of our extended hockey family now.

Catch you at the rink,

Fenix Publishing

Want **FREE BOOKS** for the rest of your LIFE?

Join our VIP club now by scanning the QR code to get **FREE** access to all our future books or enter this link: bit.ly/Free-Hockey-Books into your search browser.

We **ONLY** send you an email when we launch a **NEW BOOK. NO SPAM.** Never. Ever!

Just an email with **YOUR 100% OFF COUPON CODE.**

REFERENCES

Alex Ovechkin. (n.d.). NHL. https://www.nhl.com/capitals/player/alex-ovechkin-8471214

The Allard Foundation. (n.d.). *Dr. Charles Allard*. https://allardfoundation.com/about/allard

Associated Press. (2008a, May 9). *U.S., Canada, Sweden win at hockey worlds*. ESPN. https://africa.espn.com/olympics/news/story?id=3387594

Associated Press. (2008b, June 3). *Sykora upends Wings in third overtime to extend Cup finals*. ESPN. https://www.espn.com/nhl/recap/_/gameId/280602005

Associated Press. (2009, June 7). *Red Wings punish Fleury, Penguins to take 3-2 lead in finals*. ESPN. https://www.espn.com/nhl/recap/_/gameId/290606005

Associated Press. (2010, May 31). Blackhawks' Hossa tries to avoid forgettable hat trick in Stanley Cup finals. *The New York Times*. https://www.nytimes.com/2010/06/01/sports/hockey/01hossa.html

Associated Press. (2016, April 1). Florida Panthers penalized for too many rats on the ice. *The Guardian*. https://www.theguardian.com/sport/2016/apr/01/florida-panthers-penalized-too-many-rats-on-the-ice

Associated Press. (2023-a, June 25). Connor Bedard broke windows and records in becoming the NHL draft's presumptive no. 1 pick. *U. S. News & World Report*. https://www.usnews.com/news/sports/articles/2023-06-25/connor-bedard-broke-windows-and-records-in-becoming-the-nhl-drafts-presumptive-no-1-pick

The Associated Press. (2023-b, July 17). Chicago Blackhawks and No. 1 overall draft pick Connor Bedard agree to 3-year contract. *The Associated Press*. https://apnews.com/article/blackhawks-connor-bedard-a7f013eedd32eb3148c8b34f13120080

Attfield, P. (2024, February 23). Mark Messier says his greatest achievement might be ahead of him. *The Globe and Mail*. https://www.theglobeandmail.com/sports/article-mark-messier-says-his-greatest-achievement-might-be-ahead-of-him/

Augustyn, A. (2024a, March 31). Jaromir Jagr. In *Encyclopedia Britannica*. Retrieved April 19, 2024 https://www.britannica.com/biography/Jaromir-Jagr

Augustyn, A. (2024b, May 3). Florida Panthers. In *Encyclopedia Britannica*.. Retrieved May 4, 2024 https://www.britannica.com/topic/Florida-Panthers

Augustyn, A. (2024c, May 4). Edmonton Oilers. In *Encyclopedia Britannica*. Retrieved May 4, 2024 https://www.britannica.com/topic/Edmonton-Oilers

Bailey, D. (2023, November 25). *Sidelines: Think it can't get any worse for the Patriots? In the early '90s, it was far, far worse*. Centralmaine.com. https://www.centralmaine.com/2023/11/25/sidelines-think-it-cant-get-any-worse-for-the-patriots-in-the-early-90s-it-was-far-far-worse/

Baldoni, J. (2016, June 16). Gordie Howe: A life well-remembered. *Forbes*. https://www.forbes.com/sites/johnbaldoni/2016/06/15/gordie-howe-a-life-well-remembered/?sh=76df85292ba9

Bengel, C. (2023, February 6). *Jaromir Jagr scores 1,099th career goal, breaks Wayne Gretzky's combined goals record*. CBSSports.com. https://www.cbssports.com/nhl/news/jaromir-jagr-scores-1099th-career-goal-breaks-wayne-gretzkys-combined-goals-record

Biography.com Editors & Piccotti, T. (2023, October 19). *Alex Ovechkin*. Biography. https://www.biography.com/athletes/alex-ovechkin

Blackburn, P. (2016, October 20). *How Jaromir Jagr may have manipulated the 1990 NHL draft in his favor*. Fox Sports. https://www.foxsports.com/stories/nhl/how-jaromir-jagr-may-have-manipulated-the-1990-nhl-draft-in-his-favor

Bob Baun. (n.d.). NHL. https://www.nhl.com/player/bob-baun-8445036

Bobby Orr. (n.d.). NHL.com. https://www.nhl.com/player/bobby-orr-8450070

Bobby Orr biography. (n.d.). Www.bobbyorr.com. https://www.bobbyorr.com/Bobby-Orr-Biography-Page-01-W2.aspx

Boston Bruins playoff history. (n.d.). Champs or Chumps. https://champsorchumps.us/team/nhl/boston-bruins

BOTWC Staff. (2023, January 19). 6 important things you should know about Willie O'Ree, the first Black hockey player. Because of Them We Can. https://www.becauseofthemwecan.com/blogs/botwc-firsts/6-important-things-you-should-know-about-willie-o-ree-the-first-black-hockey-player

Brooks, H. (n.d.). Herb Brooks quotes. Herb Brooks Foundation. https://www.herbbrooksfoundation.com/herbbrooksquotes

Caldwell, D. (2002a, September 18). Hockey: Weindhandl's bid with the Isles gains speed. The New York Times. https://www.nytimes.com/2002/09/18/sports/hockey-weindhandl-s-bid-with-the-isles-gains-speed.html

Caldwell, D. (2002b, November 29). Hockey: Weindhandl finally makes an impression. The New York Times. https://www.nytimes.com/2002/11/29/sports/hockey-weindhandl-finally-makes-an-impression.html

Canadiana. (2020, February 4). 10 things you may not know about Willie O'Ree. The Royal Canadian Mint. https://www.mint.ca/en-us/blog/10-things-you-may-not-know-about-willie-oree

Cannella, S. (2004, July 5). Cap in hand: Top pick Alexander Ovechkin could break into Washington's lineup. Sports Illustrated Vault. https://vault.si.com/vault/2004/07/05/cap-in-hand-top-pick-alexander-ovechkin-could-break-into-washingtons-lineup

Caple, J. (2015, February 19). 'Red Army' tells the brutal and tragic story of the Soviet hockey program. ESPN. https://www.espn.com/blog/olympics/post/_/id/4445/red-army-tells-the-brutal-and-tragic-story-of-the-soviet-hockey-program

Castrovince, A. (2023, December 25). The 'Curse of the Bambino,' explained. Major League Baseball (MLB). https://www.mlb.com/news/curse-of-the-bambino

Chappell, B. (2022, January 19). Willie O'Ree's hockey jersey is retired, 64 years after he broke NHL color barrier. NPR. https://www.npr.org/2022/01/19/1074039448/willie-oree-hockey-jersey-retired-nhl-color-barrier

Chesnokov, D. (2014, November 24). The life and legacy of Viktor Tikhonov. Yahoo Sports. https://sports.yahoo.com/blogs/nhl-puck-daddy/the-life-and-legacy-of-viktor-tikhonov-231905628.html

Chicago Blackhawks. (2022, November 20). Marian Hossa Jersey Retirement Ceremony (FULL SPEECH) | Chicago Blackhawks [Video]. YouTube. https://www.youtube.com/watch?v=eHbOoP5gvbw

Chris. (2023, October 30). What's the definition of a Gordie Howe Hat Trick? GoonBlog.com. https://www.goonblog.com/2023/10/whats-a-gordie-howe-hat-trick/

Clarendon, D. (2024, February 19). Detroit Red Wings fans keep throwing octopuses on the ice — Here's why. Distractify. https://www.distractify.com/p/why-do-they-throw-octopus-on-the-ice-in-hockey

Commito, M. (2018). Hockey 365: Daily stories from the ice. Dundurn. https://books.google.co.za/books?id=mDY_DwAAQBAJ&dq=how+many+periods+were+played+during+the+334+club+match&source=gbs_navlinks_s

Connor Bedard. (n.d.). NHL. https://www.nhl.com/blackhawks/player/connor-bedard-8484144

Creamer, C. (2021, January 18). NHL clubs add Willie O'Ree helmet logo celebrating equality. SportsLogos.net News. https://news.sportslogos.net/2021/01/18/nhl-clubs-add-willie-oree-helmet-logo-celebrating-equality/hockey-2/

Crechiolo, M. (2024, February 16). Revisiting Jagr's rookie year. Pittsburghpenguins.com. NHL. https://www.nhl.com/penguins/news/revisiting-jagr-s-rookie-year

References

References

References
References

REFERENCES

References
References
References
References

References
References
References
References

References

References
References
References
References
References
References

References
References

References

Curtis, C. (2016, June 10). Remembering when Gordie Howe suited up for a pro hockey game at the age of 69. *USA Today*. https://ftw.usatoday.com/2016/06/gordie-howe-mr-hockey-detroit-vipers

Dater, A. (2006, October 2). Dangerous curve ahead. *The Denver Post*. https://www.denverpost.com/2006/10/02/dangerous-curve-ahead/

Davidson, N. (2023, August 15). *Bobby Baun, who scored OT goal on broken leg to win 1964 Stanley Cup, dead at 86*. CBC. https://www.cbc.ca/sports/hockey/nhl/bobby-baun-death-maple-leafs-stanley-cup-nhl-1.6936604

Dominik Hasek - Player category. (n.d.). Hockey Hall of Fame. https://www.hhof.com/induction_archives/ind14Hasek.shtml

Donahue, B. (2022, September 23). *The life and career Of Ray Bourque (Story)*. Pro Hockey History. https://www.prohockeyhistory.com/ray-bourque/

Donahue, B. (2023, December 15). *The life and career Of Mark Messier (Story)*. Pro Hockey History. https://www.prohockeyhistory.com/mark-messier/

Donahue, B. (2024, February 17). *The life and career Of Dominik Hasek (Story)*. Pro Hockey History. https://www.prohockeyhistory.com/dominik-hasek/

Doug Jarvis. (n.d.). NHL. https://www.nhl.com/player/doug-jarvis-8448254

The Editors of Encyclopædia Britannica. (n.d.-a). Gordie Howe. In *Encyclopedia Britannica*. Retrieved April 1, 2024 https://www.britannica.com/biography/Gordie-Howe

The Editors of Encyclopædia Britannica. (n.d.-b). Wayne Gretzky. In *Encyclopædia Britannica*. Retrieved April 1, 2024 https://www.britannica.com/biography/Wayne-Gretzky

Edmonton Oilers. (n.d.). Team Name Origin. https://teamnameorigin.com/nhl/nickname/edmonton-oilers

Edmonton Oilers: 1983-84 to 1989-90. (n.d.). Hockey Hall of Fame. https://www.hhof.com/hockeypedia/edmontonoilers_8384_8990.html

Edmonton Oilers Turtle Island logo collection. (n.d.). ICE District Authentics. https://www.icedistrictauthentics.com/collections/turtle-island-logo-collection

Elite Prospects. (n.d.). *About Elite Prospects*. https://www.eliteprospects.com/about

Elliott, H. (2014, November 24). Viktor Tikhonov dies at 84; Soviet coach who lost in 'Miracle on Ice'. *Los Angeles Times*. https://www.latimes.com/local/obituaries/la-me-viktor-tikhonov-20141125-story.html

Encyclopedia.com. (n.d.-a). Gordie Howe. In *Encyclopedia.com*. Retrieved April 3, 2024 https://www.encyclopedia.com/people/sports-and-games/sports-biographies/gordie-howe

Encyclopedia.com. (n.d.-b). Mikita, Stan. In *Encyclopedia.com*. Retrieved April 3, 2024 https://www.encyclopedia.com/sports/encyclopedias-almanacs-transcripts-and-maps/mikita-stan

Evelhoch, E. (2020, October 23). *'Of Miracles and Men' offers rare views of Soviet era hockey team*. The Channels. https://www.thechannels.org/ae/2020/10/23/of-miracles-and-men-offers-rare-views-of-soviet-era-hockey-team/

The evolution of the curved hockey stick. (n.d.). HockeySkillsTraining.com. https://www.hockeyskillstraining.com/the-evolution-of-the-curved-hockey-stick/

Fan Arch. (2024, February 12). *The top 10 tallest players in NHL history*. https://fanarch.com/blogs/fan-arch/the-top-10-tallest-players-in-nhl-history

Fischler, S. (2024, January 16). *Story of '334 Club' lives forever in Devils lore*. NHL. https://www.nhl.com/news/story-of-334-club-lives-forever-in-new-jersey-devils-lore

Fischler, S. I., Eskenazi, G., & Fischler, S. W. (n.d.). Ice hockey. In *Encyclopædia Britannica*. Retrieved April 3, 2024 https://www.britannica.com/sports/ice-hockey

Freeborn, J. (n.d.). Willie O'Ree. In *Encyclopedia Britannica*. Retrieved April 3, 2024 https://www.britannica.com/biography/Willie-ORee

From News Services. (1998, November 28). Messier touts NHL greats. *The Washington Post*. https://www.washingtonpost.com/archive/sports/1998/11/29/messier-touts-nhl-greats/0b2aecf7-0364-47e0-93c0-877324d2b45d/

Ganzi, J. (2024, April 22). *Florida Panthers and the history of the rats*. The Hockey Writers. https://thehockeywriters.com/florida-panthers-and-the-history-of-the-rats/

Gard, J. (2022, January 25). *A tribute to the NHL's ironman – Doug Jarvis*. Today's Northumberland. https://todaysnorthumberland.ca/2022/01/25/a-tribute-to-the-nhls-ironman-doug-jarvis/

Gipe, K. (2024, March 30). *History of the Houston Aeros*. The Hockey Writers. https://thehockeywriters.com/houston-aeros-wha/

Gipson, J. (2017, April 17). What Wayne Gretzky's father teaches us about securing talent. *The James Allen Companies, Inc. blog*. https://jamesallenco.com/what-wayne-gretzkys-father-teaches-us-about-securing-talent/

Girshin, N. (2022, March 1). *The rise and fall of Soviet hockey*. Tea and Hockey. https://teaandhockey.substack.com/p/the-rise-and-fall-of-soviet-hockey

Gordie Howe. (n.d.-a). HockeyDB.com. https://www.hockeydb.com/ihdb/stats/pdisplay.php?pid=2378

Gordie Howe. (n.d.-b). NHL.com. https://www.nhl.com/player/gordie-howe-8448000

Goss, N. (2013, August 9). *How the Wayne Gretzky trade changed hockey in the United States*. Bleacher Report. https://bleacherreport.com/articles/1731020-how-the-wayne-gretzky-trade-changed-hockey-in-the-united-states

Greenawalt, T. (2022, June 27). *Tampa Bay Lightning's Corey Perry loses 3rd Stanley Cup Final in three years*. Yahoo Sports. https://sports.yahoo.com/tampa-bay-lightnings-corey-perry-lost-3rd-stanley-cup-final-in-three-year-134718364.html

Gretz, A. (2022, January 25). *PHT Time Machine: When Doug Jarvis became the NHL's ironman*. NBC Sports. https://www.nbcsports.com/nhl/news/pht-time-machine-when-doug-jarvis-became-the-nhls-ironman

Gretzky's story. (n.d.). Gretzky.com. https://gretzky.com/bio.php

Grill, K. (2016, July 27). *The worldwide growth of ice hockey*. CoachUp. http://www.coachup.com/nation/articles/ice-hockey-growth

Gulitti, T. (2017, October 28). *Hockey Fights Cancer sparked by 'call to arms' 19 years ago*. NHL. https://www.nhl.com/news/hockey-fights-cancer-sparked-19-years-ago-292282984

Gulitti, T. (2022, December 14). *Howe's 801st NHL goal forgotten by many with Ovechkin closing in*. NHL.com. https://www.nhl.com/news/gordie-howe-801-nhl-goal-almost-forgotten-with-alex-ovechkin-one-away-338781086

Gulitti, T. (2024a, February 16). *Jagr discusses love of Pittsburgh with NHL.com ahead of number retirement*. NHL.com. https://www.nhl.com/news/gordie-howe-801-nhl-goal-almost-forgotten-with-alex-ovechkin-one-away-338781086

Gulitti, T. (2024b, February 18). *Jagr's No. 68 retired by Penguins in 'great day' for legend*. NHL. https://www.nhl.com/news/jaromir-jagr-number-68-retired-by-pittsburgh-penguins

Hauer, N. (2019, March 6). *Mattias Weinhandl: A born sniper becomes a business angel*. Kontinental Hockey League (KHL). https://en.khl.ru/news/2019/03/06/434405.html

Hershey re-establishes Teddy Bear Toss record. (2024, January 7). TheAHL.com. https://theahl.com/hershey-re-establishes-teddy-bear-toss-record

Himes, C. (n.d.). *Willie O'Ree continues to inspire youth & promote diversity*. Pittsburgh Penguins Foundation. https://www.pittsburghpenguinsfoundation.org/story/willie-oree-continues-inspire-youth-promote-diversity/

History.com Editors. (2024, February 21). *U.S. hockey team beats the Soviets in the "Miracle on ice"*. HISTORY. https://www.history.com/this-day-in-history/u-s-hockey-team-makes-miracle-on-ice

Hockey players, stats and transactions. (n.d.). Elite Prospects. https://www.eliteprospects.com/

Hockey Training. (2023, January 11). *Top hand strength is [key]* [Video]. TikTok.
https://www.tiktok.com/@hockeytraining.com/video/7187386825437138181

@hockeytraining. (2023). *Bedard's Broken Wrist* [Video]. YouTube.
https://www.youtube.com/shorts/MXZAsJn4U0A

Hooley, E. (2022, November 20). Photos: Marián Hossa's No. 81 retired by Chicago Blackhawks.
Chicago Tribune. https://www.chicagotribune.com/2022/11/20/photos-marin-hossas-no-81-
retired-by-chicago-blackhawks/

Howes, N. (2023, January 22). *The New Jersey blizzard that shut down a city, but opened the 334 Club.*
The Weather Network.
https://www.theweathernetwork.com/en/news/weather/forecasts/this-day-in-weather-
history-january-22-1987-the-334-club

The Ironman: Doug Jarvis. (2020, July 16). Peterborough Petes. https://chl.ca/ohl-petes/the-ironman-
doug-jarvis/

Jaromir Jagr. (n.d.). NHL. https://www.nhl.com/player/jaromir-jagr-8448208

Javelin Sports. (2022, October 3). 100 Surprising Sports Facts That You Never Would've Guessed.
Javelin Sports. https://www.javelinsportsinc.com/posts/100-surprising-sports-facts-that-you-
never-wouldve-guessed

Jesse. (2022, July 6). Top 10 amazing facts about Bobby Orr. *Discover Walks Blog.*
https://www.discoverwalks.com/blog/history/top-10-amazing-facts-about-bobby-orr/

Johnson, D. (2023, November 21). *Bobby Orr's flying goal.* The Hockey Writers.
https://thehockeywriters.com/bobby-orr-flying-goal-iconic/

Kauchak, G. (2022, November 18). *Hossa: My journey from Trencin to the Hall of Fame* (Book Review).
The Hockey Writers. https://thehockeywriters.com/marian-hossa-journey-from-trencin-to-the-
hall-of-fame-book-review/

Kent, D. (2024, March 28). *A list of every retired national hockey league number by team.* Big Shot
Hockey. https://bshockey.com/a-list-of-every-retired-national-hockey-league-number/

Kiddle. (2024, January 23). Zdeno Chára facts for kids. *Kiddle Encyclopedia.*
https://kids.kiddle.co/Zdeno_Ch%C3%A1ra

LeBrun, P. (2009, July 1). *Hossa, Blackhawks agree on deal.* ESPN.
https://www.espn.com/nhl/news/story?id=4300131

Luedeke, K. A. (2018, August 9). *Thoughts on "the trade"—30 years ago today Wayne Gretzky to Los
Angeles helped to transform hockey in the USA.* Scoutingpost.
https://scoutingpost.com/2018/08/09/thoughts-on-the-trade-30-years-ago-today-wayne-
gretzkys-trade-to-los-angeles-helped-to-transform-hockey-in-the-usa/

Marian Hossa. (n.d.). NHL. https://www.nhl.com/player/marian-hossa-8466148

Mark Messier. (n.d.). NHL.com. https://www.nhl.com/player/mark-messier-8449573

.Mark Messier - Player category. (n.d.). Hockey Hall of Fame.
https://www.hhof.com/induction_archives/ind07Messier.shtml

Mattias Weinhandl. (n.d.-a). Eurohockey.com. https://www.eurohockey.com/player/10062-mattias-
weinhandl.html

Mattias Weinhandl. (n.d.-b). HockeyDB.com.
https://www.hockeydb.com/ihdb/stats/pdisplay.php?pid=45045

Mattias Weinhandl. (2014, April 4). GreatestHockeyLegends.com.
http://www.greatesthockeylegends.com/2014/04/mattias-weinhandl.html

Mayo Clinic Staff. (2022, March 8). *Hodgkin's lymphoma (Hodgkin's disease)*. Mayo Clinic. https://www.mayoclinic.org/diseases-conditions/hodgkins-lymphoma/symptoms-causes/syc-20352646

McArdle, T. (2020, January 26). *Ontario Reign's Martin Frk breaks Zdeno Chara's hardest shot record in AHL skills competition*. The Sporting News. https://www.sportingnews.com/us/nhl/news/ontario-reign-martin-frk-breaks-zdeno-charas-hardest-shot-record-in-ahl-skills-competition/8hg9jjl9jykt1t5ryr1mwmh5j

McGillivray, B. (n.d.). Edmonton: Alberta, Canada. In *Encyclopædia Britannica*. Retrieved May 4, 2024 https://www.britannica.com/place/Edmonton-Alberta

Milbert, N. (2018, August 7). Blackhawks great Stan Mikita dies at 78: 'He was hard-working. He was unselfish. He was a superstar'. *Chicago Tribune*. https://www.chicagotribune.com/2018/08/07/blackhawks-great-stan-mikita-dies-at-78-he-was-hard-working-he-was-unselfish-he-was-a-superstar/

Miller, M. (2024, February 17). *Jaromir Jagr admits he told Canucks not to draft him*. The Hockey News. https://thehockeynews.com/nhl/vancouver-canucks/news/jaromir-jagr-admits-he-told-canucks-not-to-draft-him

Mondal, A. (2023a, August 10). *Did Wayne Gretzky ever win a Stanley Cup with the Los Angeles Kings?* Sportskeeda. https://www.sportskeeda.com/us/nhl/news-did-wayne-gretzky-ever-win-stanley-cup-los-angeles-kings

Mondal, A. (2023b, September 2). *What is Wayne Gretzky's illness? Understanding NHL GOAT's battle with chronic pain*. Sportskeeda. https://www.sportskeeda.com/us/nhl/news-what-wayne-gretzky-s-illness-understanding-nhl-goat-s-battle-chronic-pain

Murphy, B. (2022, November 18). *Phil Kessel Ironman streak: How the Golden Knights forward's NHL record stacks up against all-time leaders in NFL, MLB and NBA*. https://www.sportingnews.com/ca/nhl/news/phil-kessel-ironman-streak-nhl-record-against-all-time-leaders-nfl-mlb-nba/r7up3svoh56y3trhbefrvt1b

Murphy, B. (2023, April 29). *How Mark Messier's Game 6 guarantee win vs. Devils became a rallying cry for the '94 Rangers NHL playoff run*. The Sporting News. https://www.sportingnews.com/us/nhl/news/mark-messier-guarantee-rangers-predicted-1994-playoff-victory-devils/eqxd0zr7xuebfhpmj32uzll4

Naylor, D. (2003, March 15). Hockey all in the family for Hossas. *The Globe and Mail*. https://www.theglobeandmail.com/sports/hockey-all-in-the-family-for-hossas/article1011581/

NBC Sports Boston. (2021, June 8). *Before the Duckboats: The Ray Bourque City Hall rally* [Video]. YouTube. https://www.youtube.com/watch?v=c_fi_WdAW8w

New York Times. (1993, January 17). Gretzky, Messier close despite distance. *Chicago Tribune*. https://www.chicagotribune.com/1993/01/17/gretzky-messier-close-despite-distance/

NHL. (2010, June 9). *Blackhawks win Stanley Cup in OT, beat Flyers in Game 6* [Video]. YouTube. https://www.youtube.com/watch?v=PO5SnehKowM

NHL. (2017, May 25). *Memories: Messier guarantees Game 6 victory* [Video]. YouTube. https://www.youtube.com/watch?app=desktop&v=viIVXg0AhOI

NHL Public Relations. (2024, February 18). *#NHLStats ahead of Penguins retiring Jaromir Jagr's no. 68*. NHL.com. https://media.nhl.com/public/news/17732

NHLPA Staff. (2024, January 13). *Ovechkin hosts seventh American Special Hockey Association clinic*. National Hockey League Players' Association. https://www.nhlpa.com/news/1-22604/ovechkin-hosts-seventh-american-special-hockey-association-clinic

The 1980 U.S. Olympic team. (n.d.). U.S. Hockey Hall of Fame. https://www.ushockeyhalloffame.com/page/show/831562-the-1980-u-s-olympic-team

Nivision, A. (2023, August 15). *Bobby Baun, legendary Toronto Maple Leafs defenseman, dies at 86.* CBS Sports. https://www.cbssports.com/nhl/news/bobby-baun-legendary-toronto-maple-leafs-defenseman-dies-at-86/

OTD: Mario Lemieux born in Montréal. (2021, October 5). Canadian Coin News. https://canadiancoinnews.com/mario-lemieux-born-in-montreal-1965/

Paine, N. (2023, March 2). *How Mario Lemieux beat cancer — And started a comeback for the ages.* FiveThirtyEight. https://fivethirtyeight.com/features/how-mario-lemieux-beat-cancer-and-started-a-comeback-for-the-ages/

Patrick Marleau. (n.d.). NHL.com. https://www.nhl.com/player/patrick-marleau-8466139

Petersen, W. (2022, June 9). *Iconic moment: 21 years ago today Sakic handed Stanley Cup to Bourque.* Denver Sports. https://denversports.com/2098825/iconic-moment-21-years-ago-today-sakic-handed-stanley-cup-to-bourque/

Plian, L. (2024, February 29). *The towering legacy of Zdeno Chara in the NHL.* Articles Factory. https://www.articlesfactory.com/articles/sports/charas-season-in-ice-hockey.html

Politi, S. (2017, January 22). *Remembering the night 334 fans watched the Devils play in a blizzard 30 years ago.* Nj.com. https://www.nj.com/devils/2017/01/the_blizzard_game_remembering_the_strangest_night.html

ThePostGame Staff. (2014, February 21). Players from USA hockey's 1980 'miracle on ice' team who competed in the NHL. *ThePostGame.* http://www.thepostgame.com/blog/list/201402/1980-us-olympic-hockey-team-miracle-ice-lake-placid-nhl

Predators. (2023, March 7). *Tiki Tikhonov - New Piedmont girls director.* Piedmont Predators Hockey. https://www.piedmonthockeyclub.com/news_article/show/1263550

Puckstruck. (2019, February 3). *On this night in 1962: Boom goes the leafs' bench.* https://puckstruck.com/2019/02/03/on-this-night-in-1962-boom-goes-the-leafs-bench/

Quinn, J. (2020, April 18). *Celtics Wire evening trivia - April 18: Boston's forgettable 1990s.* Celtics Wire. https://celticswire.usatoday.com/2020/04/18/nba-boston-celtics-vs-chicago-bulls-preview-jan-4-4/

Rappleye, T. (2019, June 11). *The shot of a lifetime.* FloHockey. https://www.flohockey.tv/articles/6517190-the-shot-of-a-lifetime

Rasbach, N. (1988, August 10). *Canadians stunned by Gretzky trade.* UPI. https://www.upi.com/Archives/1988/08/10/Canadians-stunned-by-Gretzky-trade/1356587188800/

Rattner, N. (2024, March 21). *Sidney Crosby vs Alexander Ovechkin.* Elite Prospects. https://www.eliteprospects.com/page/sidney-crosby-vs-alexander-ovechkin

Ray Bourque. (n.d.). NHL. https://www.nhl.com/player/ray-bourque-8445621

Ray Bourque Foundation. (n.d.). *About Ray Bourque.* https://bourquefamilyfoundation.org/about-ray/

Ray Bourque - Player category. (n.d.). Hockey Hall of Fame. https://www.hhof.com/induction_archives/ind04Bourque.shtml

Robbins, M. (n.d.). *Homemade Pierogi.* King Arthur Baking Company. https://www.kingarthurbaking.com/recipes/homemade-pierogi-recipe

Robinson, A. (2015, November 19). Stanley Cup Finals: Near-miracle finish falls short for Pens. *New Castle News.* https://www.ncnewsonline.com/sports/stanley-cup-finals-near-miracle-finish-falls-short-for-pens/article_c65d662a-047e-5407-b37b-69f2974d412e.html

The role of aerodynamics in ice hockey: How stick design affects shot accuracy. (2023, October 25). *AYCANE.* https://aycane.com/blogs/news/the-role-of-aerodynamics-in-ice-hockey-how-stick-design-affects-shot-accuracy

Russo, E. (2021, January7). *The history of the Bruins captaincy*. NHL.com. https://www.nhl.com/bruins/news/the-history-of-the-bruins-captaincy-320038260

Schwartz, L. (n.d.-a). *Mario was super despite the obstacles*. ESPN.com. https://www.espn.com/classic/biography/s/Lemieux_Mario.html

Schwartz, L. (n.d.-b). *Orr brought more offense to defense*. ESPN.com. https://www.espn.com/sportscentury/features/00016391.html

Séguin, C. (2024, April 8). *Landon DuPont becomes the ninth Exceptional Status Player in CHL history*. The Canadian Hockey League (CHL). https://chl.ca/video/landon-dupont-becomes-the-ninth-exceptional-status-player-in-chl-history

Seide, J. (2024, January 18). *Mark Messier – NHL legend and 6-time Stanley Cup winner*. The Hockey Writers. https://thehockeywriters.com/mark-messier-nhl-legend/

Sharma, A. (2011, July 2). *"Title-Town" --- How Boston became the city of champions (Part 1: Patriots)*. Bleacher Report. https://bleacherreport.com/articles/755866-title-town-how-boston-became-the-city-of-champions

Shilton, K. (2022, January 18). *'We will never let his name die': How NHL players have been inspired by Willie O'Ree*. ESPN.com. https://africa.espn.com/nhl/story/_/id/33085109/we-never-let-name-die-how-nhl-players-inspired-willie-oree

Shuster, S. (2014, February 14). *It's time to get over the 'miracle on ice'*. Time. https://time.com/8473/its-time-to-get-over-the-miracle-on-ice/

Sidney Crosby. (n.d.). NHL. https://www.nhl.com/penguins/player/sidney-crosby-8471675

Sidney Crosby Hockey School. (n.d.). *The Sidney Crosby Foundation*. https://sidneycrosbyhockeyschool.com

Snyder, L. (2009, October 1). Raymond Jean Bourque. In *The Canadian Encyclopedia*. Retrieved April 19, 2024 https://www.thecanadianencyclopedia.ca/en/article/raymond-jean-bourque

Spezialetti, S. (2023, January 12). *30 Years Ago Today...* Mario Lemieux Foundation. https://mariolemieux.org/30-years-ago-today/

The Sports Hayes. (2014, June 30). *Boston Celtics all-decade teams: The 1990s*. Celtics Life. https://www.celticslife.com/2014/06/boston-celtics-all-decade-teams-1990s.html

Sportsnet. (2018, February 21). *Zdeno Chara's NHL beginnings started in Prince George* [Video]. YouTube. https://www.youtube.com/watch?v=2rCjQ-gP-zU

Stan Mikita. (n.d.). HockeyDB.com. https://www.hockeydb.com/ihdb/stats/pdisplay.php?pid=3711

Stan Mikita (1940-2018). (n.d.). IMDb. Retrieved March 16, 2024 https://www.imdb.com/name/nm0586545/

Stan Mikita. (n.d.). StatMuse. https://www.statmuse.com/nhl/player/stan-mikita-4729

Stewart, J. D. M. (2017, June 13). Sidney Crosby. In *the Canadian Encyclopedia*. https://www.thecanadianencyclopedia.ca/en/article/sidney-crosby

Straight talk about the beginning of the curved hockey stick. (n.d.). Pro Stock Hockey. https://www.prostockhockey.com/sticks/who-made-the-first-curved-hockey-stick

Stubbs, D. (2023, August 15). *Baun 'did anything he could' to help Maple Leafs win, Keon says*. NHL. https://www.nhl.com/news/bobby-baun-important-part-of-toronto-maple-leafs-stanley-cup-titles-345598304

Team Soviet Union - Olympics - Lake Placid 1980 - Player stats. (n.d.). QuantHockey. https://www.quanthockey.com/olympics/en/teams/team-soviet-union-players-1980-olympics-stats.html

teamhoytofficial. (2023, May 24). *Great day yesterday with Zdeno Chara at Longboards in Salem supporting both The Hoyt Foundation and the Thomas E. Smith Foundation* [Photographs]. Instagram. https://www.instagram.com/p/C45wP9XrlTt/?img_index=1

Ted Talks Hockey. (n.d.). *Ten NHL brother combinations (National Hockey League)*. https://tedtalkshockey.com/2021/12/06/ten-nhl-brother-combinations-national-hockey-league/

THW Archives. (2023, November 24). *Remembering Viktor Tikhonov: A hockey legend*. The Hockey Writers. https://thehockeywriters.com/remembering-viktor-tikhonov-a-hockey-legend/

TSN. (2023a, January 4). *Connor Bedard's shot broke away from the competition when he was 13* [Video]. Facebook. https://www.facebook.com/watch/?v=878502120006470

TSN. (2023b, January 9). *How Connor Bedard developed the NHL's next best shot* [Video]. YouTube. https://www.youtube.com/watch?v=ShFJ7MZeIU4

2023 NHL Global Series - Melbourne. (n.d.). NHL.com. https://www.nhl.com/events/2023-nhl-global-series-melbourne

USA Today Sports. (2020, February 21). *Mike Eruzione reveals untold stories from 'miracle on ice' Olympic hockey game* [Video]. YouTube. https://www.youtube.com/watch?v=d8ozRzU1mO8

Vanderberg, Z. (2011, February 5). *Czech mate: The top ten Czech Republic NHL players of all time*. Bleacher Report. https://bleacherreport.com/articles/595909-czech-mate-the-top-ten-czech-nhl-players-of-all-time

Vanstone, R. (2023, January 3). Connor Bedard: From a young age, he was determined to be a hockey star. *Toronto Sun*. https://torontosun.com/sports/hockey/connor-bedard-from-a-young-age-he-was-determined-to-be-a-hockey-star

Waldstein, D. (2023, February 28). The 51-year-old hockey star who won't quit. *The New York Times*. https://www.nytimes.com/2023/02/28/sports/hockey/jaromir-jagr-czech-extraliga.html

Washington Post Staff. (2014, November 25). Viktor Tikhonov, Soviet hockey coach who led team to three gold medals, dies at 84. *The Washington Post*. https://www.washingtonpost.com/sports/viktor-tikhonov-soviet-hockey-coach-who-led-team-to-three-gold-medals-dies-at-84/2014/11/25/332fba10-74cd-11e4-a755-e32227229e7b_story.html

Wayne. (2019). *Culture*. OilersNation. https://oilersnation.com/news/culture-and-the-edmonton-oilers

Wayne Gretzky. (n.d.-a). HockeyDB.com. https://www.hockeydb.com/ihdb/stats/pdisplay.php?pid=2035

Wayne Gretzky. (n.d.-b). NHL.com. https://www.nhl.com/player/wayne-gretzky-8447400

Wayne Gretzky. (n.d.-c). StatMuse. https://www.statmuse.com/nhl/player/wayne-gretzky-2501

W. D. "Bill" Hunter. (n.d.). Alberta Sports Hall of Fame. https://albertasportshallmembers.ca/home/profiles/385

Weekend at Bergys. (2015, January 11). *Zdeno Chara feature on 60 Minutes Sports - Showtime* [Video]. YouTube. https://www.youtube.com/watch?v=z8skxq6wWso

What is illegal curve in hockey? (2023, August 23). Hockey Monkey. https://www.hockeymonkey.com/learn/illegal-curve-hockey

What impact did Mario Lemieux have on Jaromir Jagr's career? (n.d.). Quora. https://www.quora.com/What-impact-did-Mario-Lemieux-have-on-Jaromir-Jagrs-career

Who was the youngest player to win both the mvp award in a season and the finals mvp award? (n.d.). StatMuse. https://www.statmuse.com/nhl/ask/who-was-the-youngest-player-to-win-both-the-mvp-award-and-the-finals-mvp-award

Willie O'Ree. (n.d.-a). HockeyDB.com. https://www.hockeydb.com/ihdb/stats/pdisplay.php?pid=8354

Willie O'Ree. (n.d.-b). NHL. https://www.nhl.com/player/willie-o-ree-8448064

Woooo. (2008, June 5). *2008 Stanley Cup finals: The Pittsburgh Penguins' long road to ruin*. Bleacher Report. https://bleacherreport.com/articles/27619-2008-stanley-cup-finals-the-pittsburgh-penguins-long-road-to-ruin

Zdeno Chara. (n.d.). NHL. https://www.nhl.com/player/zdeno-chara-8465009

Made in United States
Troutdale, OR
12/11/2024